Authors, Consultants, and Reviewers

MULTICULTURAL AND EDUCATIONAL
CONSULTANTS

Alma Flor Ada, Yvonne Beamer, Joyce Buckner,
Helen Gillotte, Cheryl Hudson, Narcita Medina,
Lorraine Monroe, James R. Murphy, Sylvia Peña,
Joseph B. Rubin, Ramon Santiago, Cliff Trafzer,
Hai Tran, Esther Lee Yao

LITERATURE CONSULTANTS

Ashley Bryan, Joan I. Glazer, Paul Janeczko,
Margaret H. Lippert

INTERNATIONAL CONSULTANTS

Edward B. Adams, Barbara Johnson,
Raymond L. Marshall

MUSIC AND AUDIO CONSULTANTS

John Farrell, Marilyn C. Davidson,
Vincent Lawrence, Sarah Pirtle, Susan R. Synder,
Rick and Deborah Witkowski, Eastern Sky Media
Services, Inc.

TEACHER REVIEWERS

Terry Baker, Jane Bauer, James Bedi, Nora Bickel,
Vernell Bowen, Donald Cason, Jean Chaney,
Carolyn Clark, Alan Cox, Kathryn DesCarpentrie,
Carol L. Ellis, Roberta Gale, Brenda Huffman,
Erma Inscore, Sharon Kidwell, Elizabeth Love,
Isabel Marcus, Elaine McCraney, Michelle Moraros,
Earlene Parr, Dr. Richard Potts, Jeanette Pulliam,
Michael Rubin, Henrietta Sakamaki,
Kathleen Cultron Sanders, Belinda Snow,
Dr. Jayne Steubing, Margaret Mary Sulentic,
Barbara Tate, Seretta Vincent,
Willard Waite, Barbara Wilson, Veronica York

Macmillan/McGraw-Hill

A Division of The McGraw·Hill Companies

Copyright © 2000, 1999 McGraw-Hill School Division,
a Division of the Educational and Professional
Publishing Group of The McGraw-Hill Companies, Inc.

McGraw-Hill School Division
Two Penn Plaza
New York, New York 10121
Printed in the United States of America

ISBN 0-02-185881-0 / 3, L. 9

2 3 4 5 6 7 8 9 071 03 02 01 00 99

FORM 51-126-00 (Rev. 4/90)

Spotlight on Literacy

AUTHORS

ELAINE MEI AOKI • VIRGINIA ARNOLD • JAMES FLOOD • JAMES V. HOFFMAN • DIANE LAPP

MIRIAM MARTINEZ • ANNEMARIE SULLIVAN PALINCSAR • MICHAEL PRIESTLEY • CARL B. SMITH

WILLIAM H. TEALE • JOSEFINA VILLAMIL TINAJERO • ARNOLD W. WEBB • KAREN D. WOOD

Macmillan McGraw-Hill

NEW YORK • FARMINGTON

Unit 1

COMMUNITY SPIRIT

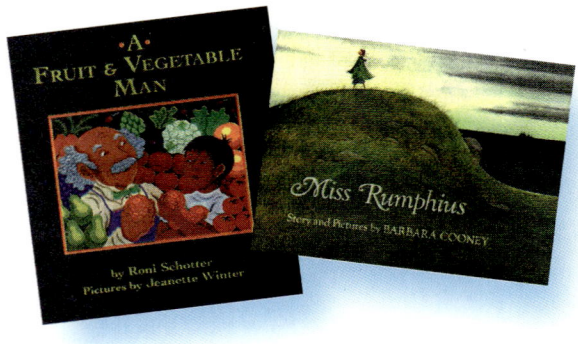

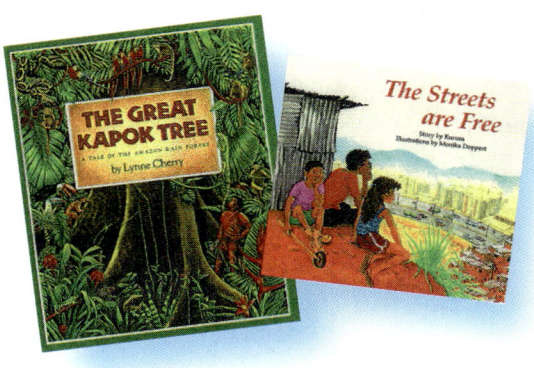

Unit 2

Forces of Nature

Unit 3

TEAMWORK

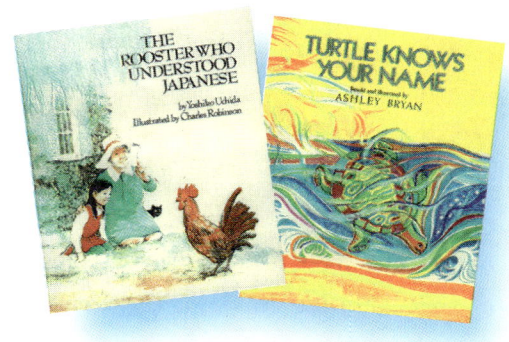

Unit 1

COMMUNITY SPIRIT

A Fruit & Vegetable Man

by Roni Schotter
illustrated by Jeanette Winter

Ruby Rubenstein was a fruit and vegetable man. His motto was "I take care." Six mornings a week, long before the sun was up, Ruby was.

"*Is it time,* Ruby?" his wife Trudy always asked from deep under the covers.

"It's time," Ruby always answered. Then he'd jump out of bed, touch his knees, then his toes, and hurry uptown to market to choose the ripest fruit and vegetables for his store.

For nearly fifty years it had been so—ever since he and Trudy first sailed across the ocean to make a new life together.

Every morning before school, Sun Ho and his sister, Young Mee, who with their family, had just flown across the sky to make a new life together, came to watch Ruby work his magic.

"Yo-ho, Mr. Ruby!" Sun Ho would call out. "Show me!"

And nodding to Sun Ho, Ruby would pile apples, tangerines, and pears in perfect pyramids, arrange grapes in diamonds, insert a head of lettuce as accent, then tuck in a bunch of broccoli or a bit of watercress for trim.

It was like seeing a great artist at work. Sun Ho felt honored to be there. "Like a painting, Mr. Ruby!" he would say shyly.

Ruby always smiled, and his smile filled Sun Ho with happiness and, deep inside, a strange feeling that was like wishing. Sun Ho watched as Ruby juggled cantaloupes, then cut them into wedges and packed them neatly in plastic. Inside Sun Ho, the feeling that was like wishing grew stronger.

"He's an artist, all right," Old Ella from up the block always said, pocketing an apple and a handful of prunes.

Ruby didn't mind. He'd just wink and utter one wonderful word: "Taste!" Then he'd offer whatever he had on special that day to Sun Ho, his sister, and anyone who wanted.

"What would we *do* without Ruby?" Mary Morrissey asked the crowd one gray afternoon. The people of Delano Street sighed and shook their heads at such a terrible thought.

"Mr. Ruby," Sun Ho said, "he's one of a kind."

Yes, everyone on Delano Street appreciated Ruby. But Ruby was getting old. Lately, when he got up to touch his knees and his toes, there was a stiffness Ruby pretended he didn't feel and a creaking Trudy pretended she didn't hear. And sometimes, though Ruby never would admit it, there was a wish that he could stay a little longer in bed with Trudy.

"Ruby," Trudy said to him one morning from under the covers. "Long ago you and I made a promise. We said if ever we got old, we'd sell the business and go to live in the mountains. *Is it time, Ruby?*"

"NO!!" Ruby thundered. And he leapt out of bed, did *twice* his usual number of exercises, and ran off to market.

As if to prove he was as young as ever, he worked especially hard at the store that day and made some of his most beautiful designs.

That afternoon, Sun Ho came by as Ruby was arranging potatoes in his own special way. Sun Ho watched as Ruby whirled them in the air and tossed them with such skill that they landed perfectly, one next to the other in a neat row.

"Yo-ho, Mr. Ruby!" Sun Ho said, filled with admiration. "Teach me?"

Proudly, Ruby grabbed an Idaho and two russets and taught Sun Ho how to juggle. Next he taught him how to pile grapefruits to keep them from falling. By the time Sun Ho's parents stopped by, Ruby had even taught Sun Ho how to work the register. Then he sat Sun Ho down and told him how, early every morning, he went to market to choose his fruit and vegetables.

"Take me!" Sun Ho pleaded, the feeling that was like wishing so big now he felt he might burst. "Please?"

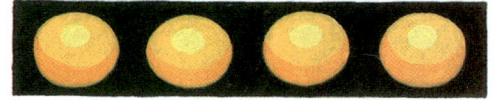

Ruby thought for only a moment. Then he spoke. "My pleasure," he announced.

So early the next day, while Venus still sparkled in the dark morning sky, Ruby took Sun Ho to market. Sun Ho had an excellent nose, and together he and Ruby sniffed out the most fragrant fruit and sampled the choicest chicory. Then Ruby showed Sun Ho how he talked and teased and argued his way to the best prices.

All the rest of that long day, Sun Ho felt special. And Ruby? He felt, well . . . tired. Whenever Trudy was busy with a customer, Ruby leaned over and pretended to tie his

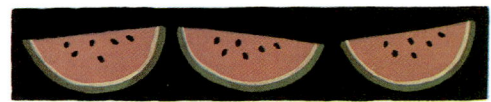

shoe, but what he did, really, was *yawn*. By afternoon,
Ruby was running out of the store every few minutes. "The
fruit!" he'd yell to Trudy. "Got to fix the fruit!" he'd say,
but once outside, what he did, really, was *sneeze*.

"To your health, Mr. Ruby," Sun Ho whispered,
sneaking him a handkerchief.

"Thank you, Mr. Sun Ho," Ruby said, quietly blowing
his nose.

That evening it began to snow on Delano Street.

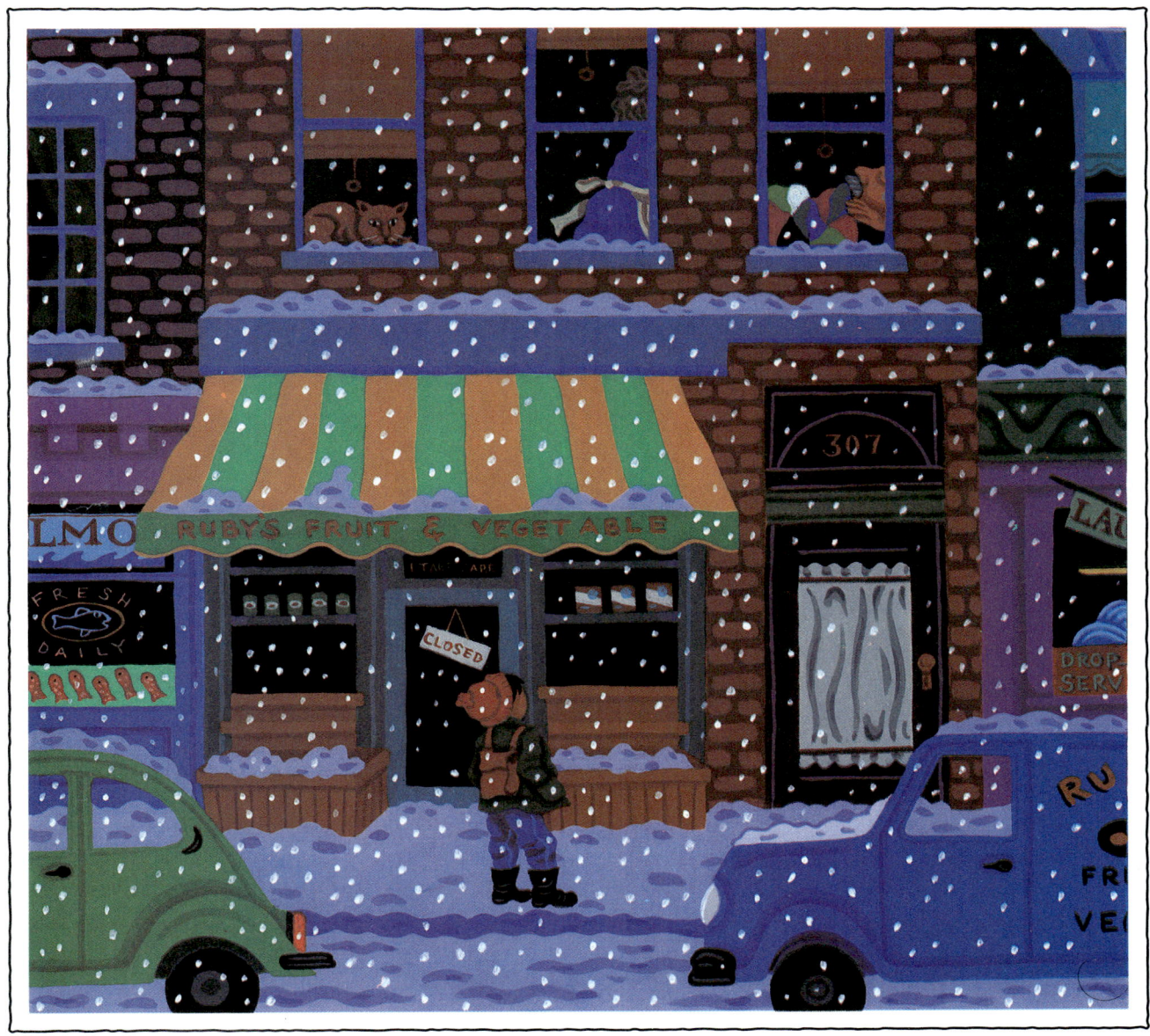

It snowed all night, and by morning the street was cold and white, the color of fresh cauliflower.

For the first time in many years, Ruby woke up feeling sick. His face was red, his forehead hot. "No work today," Trudy said. "Ruby's Fruit and Vegetable is closed until further notice." What would the people of Delano Street do without him? Ruby wondered. But he was too sick to care.

When Sun Ho arrived at the store that day and saw that it was closed, he was worried. Where was Ruby?

Upstairs in his bed, Ruby dozed, dreaming of spring and fresh apricots. Once, when he opened his eyes, Sun Ho was standing next to him . . . or was he?

"No worries," Sun Ho seemed to say. "I take care." Then as strangely as he had appeared, Sun Ho disappeared. Was Ruby dreaming?

For the next three days, for the first time in his life, Ruby was too sick to think or worry about his store. He stayed deep under the covers, enjoying Trudy's loving care, and more than that, her barley soup. On the morning of the fourth day, he felt well enough to worry. On the morning of the fifth day, a Saturday, there was no stopping him. "My store!" he shouted. Leaning on Trudy's arm, he put on his clothes. Then he rushed off to reopen.

What a surprise when he arrived! The store was open. In fact, it looked as if it had never been shut. The peppers were in pyramids, the dates in diamonds, the winter tomatoes in triangles. Sun Ho's father was helping Old Ella to a pound of carrots. Sun Ho's mother was at the register. Young Mee was polishing pears. And, in the center of it all, Sun Ho stood smiling, offering customers a taste of something new—bean sprouts!

When they saw Ruby, everyone cheered. Ruby bowed with pleasure.

"I took care, Mr. Ruby!" Sun Ho called out proudly.

"I see," Ruby answered. "You're a fruit and vegetable man, Sun Ho, like me."

Sun Ho's face turned the color of Ruby's radishes. The feeling that was like wishing was gone now. In its place was a different feeling: pride.

"*Is it time,* Ruby?" Trudy whispered.

Ruby sighed. He thought about how much he liked Sun Ho and his family and how carefully they had kept his store. He thought about the stiffness and creaking in his knees. He thought about the mountains and about Trudy's loving care. More than that, he thought about her barley soup.

"It's time," he said finally.

Now Sun Ho is a fruit and vegetable man! Every morning, long before the sun is up, long before it's time for school, Sun Ho and his family are up, ready to hurry to market to choose the ripest fruit and vegetables for their store.

And Ruby? He's still a fruit and vegetable man . . . only now he and Trudy grow their own.

MEET
RONI SCHOTTER

One of Roni Schotter's favorite childhood memories is of visiting the public library with her mother.

"I got to choose books from a special low shelf that held all the Caldecott winners. I loved everything about those books."

Schotter never lost her love of books. She worked as a children's book editor and later began writing her own stories for children.

Her first book was *A Matter of Time*. It was made into an "ABC After School Special." The program won an Emmy, an award given for excellence in television. Her book *Hanukkah!* won the 1991 National Jewish Book Award.

MEET
JEANETTE WINTER

For Jeanette Winter, working on *A Fruit & Vegetable Man* was an enjoyable experience. She says, "I have always liked the fruit and vegetable markets in New York." Winter visited many of the old markets in that city. As she often does when working on a book, she took many photographs. She used them to get ideas for her illustrations.

Winter says, "I try to tell the story with my pictures. I also try to make the sort of pictures that I would have enjoyed looking at as a child."

From Sea to

From California and the Pacific Ocean to New York and the Atlantic Ocean, people are saying it really is up to us!

Oakland, California

Students from the Glenview and La Escuelita schools created four murals of their city. But they left one thing out— litter! Why? They wanted people to see Oakland as a beautiful, litter-free place to live.

As one student, Nathaniel Gallardo, explained, "I hope that when people see our murals, they will think that these kids know how beautiful Oakland is because of the way they painted it."

Shining Sea

Courtesy of Festival at the Lake, Oakland, California.

New York, New York

In the middle of a New York City neighborhood, old tires, rusty bedsprings, and abandoned cars once covered three lots. Then the "Lot Busters" arrived. This group of neighborhood adults and children "found" a secret garden under all the junk.

The "Lot Busters" spent six months hauling away trash and preparing the lots for planting. People didn't mind the hard work, though. As Elena Maldonado said, "When you work with family and friends, even pushing a two-ton car out of a lot can be fun."

Miss Rumphius

The Lupine Lady lives in a small house overlooking the sea. In between the rocks around her house grow blue and purple and rose-colored flowers. The Lupine Lady is little and old. But she has not always been that way. I know. She is my great-aunt, and she told me so.

Once upon a time she was a little girl named Alice, who lived in a city by the sea. From the front stoop she could see the wharves and the bristling masts of tall ships. Many years ago her grandfather had come to America on a large sailing ship.

Story and Pictures by Barbara Cooney

Now he worked in the shop at the bottom of the house, making figureheads for the prows of ships, and carving Indians out of wood to put in front of cigar stores. For Alice's grandfather was an artist. He painted pictures, too, of sailing ships and places across the sea. When he was very busy, Alice helped him put in the skies.

In the evening Alice sat on her grandfather's knee and listened to his stories of faraway places. When he had finished, Alice would say, "When I grow up, I too will go to faraway places, and when I grow old, I too will live beside the sea."

"That is all very well, little Alice," said her grandfather, "but there is a third thing you must do."

"What is that?" asked Alice.

"You must do something to make the world more beautiful," said her grandfather.

"All right," said Alice. But she did not know what that could be.

In the meantime Alice got up and washed her face and ate porridge for breakfast. She went to school and came home and did her homework.

And pretty soon she was grown up.

Then my Great-aunt Alice set out to do the three things she had told her grandfather she was going to do. She left home and went to live in another city far from the sea and the salt air. There she worked in a library, dusting books and keeping them from getting mixed up, and helping people find the ones they wanted. Some of the books told her about faraway places.

People called her Miss Rumphius now.

Sometimes she went to the conservatory in the middle of the park. When she stepped inside on a wintry day, the warm moist air wrapped itself around her, and the sweet smell of jasmine filled her nose.

"This is almost like a tropical isle," said Miss Rumphius. "But not quite."

So Miss Rumphius went to a real tropical island, where people kept cockatoos and monkeys as pets. She walked on long beaches, picking up beautiful shells. One day she met the Bapa Raja, king of a fishing village.

"You must be tired," he said. "Come into my house and rest."

So Miss Rumphius went in and met the Bapa Raja's wife. The Bapa Raja himself fetched a green coconut and cut a slice off the top so that Miss Rumphius could drink the coconut water inside. Before she left, the Bapa Raja gave her a beautiful mother-of-pearl shell on which he had painted a bird of paradise and the words, "You will always remain in my heart."

"You will always remain in mine too," said Miss Rumphius.

My great-aunt Miss Alice Rumphius
climbed tall mountains where the snow
never melted. She went through jungles
and across deserts. She saw lions
playing and kangaroos jumping. And
everywhere she made friends she would
never forget. Finally she came to the
Land of the Lotus-Eaters, and there,
getting off a camel, she hurt her back.

"What a foolish thing to do," said
Miss Rumphius. "Well, I have certainly
seen faraway places. Maybe it is time to
find my place by the sea."

And it was, and she did.

From the porch of her new house
Miss Rumphius watched the sun come
up; she watched it cross the heavens
and sparkle on the water; and she saw
it set in glory in the evening. She
started a little garden among the rocks
that surrounded her house, and she
planted a few flower seeds in the
stony ground. Miss Rumphius was
almost perfectly happy.

"But there is still one more thing
I have to do," she said. "I have to do
something to make the world more
beautiful."

But what? "The world already is
pretty nice," she thought, looking out
over the ocean.

39

The next spring Miss Rumphius was not very well. Her back was bothering her again, and she had to stay in bed most of the time.

The flowers she had planted the summer before had come up and bloomed in spite of the stony ground. She could see them from her bedroom window, blue and purple and rose-colored.

"Lupines," said Miss Rumphius with satisfaction. "I have always loved lupines the best. I wish I could plant more seeds this summer so that I could have still more flowers next year."

But she was not able to.

After a hard winter spring came. Miss Rumphius was feeling much better. Now she could take walks again. One afternoon she started to go up and over the hill, where she had not been in a long time.

"I don't believe my eyes!" she cried when she got to the top. For there on the other side of the hill was

a large patch of blue and purple and rose-colored lupines!

"It was the wind," she said as she knelt in delight. "It was the wind that brought the seeds from my garden here! And the birds must have helped!"

Then Miss Rumphius had a wonderful idea!

She hurried home and got out her seed catalogues. She sent off to the very best seed house for five bushels of lupine seed.

All that summer Miss Rumphius, her pockets full of seeds, wandered over fields and headlands, sowing lupines. She scattered seeds along the highways and down the country lanes. She flung handfuls of them around the schoolhouse and back of the church. She tossed them into hollows and along stone walls.

Her back didn't hurt her any more at all.

Now some people called her That Crazy Old Lady.

The next spring there were lupines everywhere. Fields and hillsides were covered with blue and purple and rose-colored flowers. They bloomed along the highways and down the lanes. Bright patches lay around the schoolhouse and back of the

church. Down in the hollows and along the stone walls grew the beautiful flowers.

Miss Rumphius had done the third, the most difficult thing of all!

My Great-aunt Alice, Miss Rumphius, is very old now. Her hair is very white. Every year there are more and more lupines. Now they call her the Lupine Lady. Sometimes my friends stand with me outside her gate, curious to see the old, old lady who planted the fields of lupines. When she invites us in, they come slowly. They think she is the oldest woman in the world. Often she tells us stories of faraway places.

"When I grow up," I tell her, "I too will go to faraway places and come home to live by the sea."

"That is all very well, little Alice," says my aunt, "but there is a third thing you must do."

"What is that?" I ask.

"You must do something to make the world more beautiful."

"All right," I say.

But I do not know yet
        what that can be.

Meet
Barbara Cooney

There really was a woman in Maine who collected lupine seeds and "flung handfuls of them around," just as in *Miss Rumphius*. The woman wasn't exactly like the character in the book, but she provided "the seed of the idea" for Barbara Cooney. The author helped the idea grow until she had a story that was like a modern fairy tale.

People often ask Barbara Cooney how she came to write or illustrate her books. This is what she said when asked about her drawings in *Chanticleer and the Fox:* "That question is a little embarrassing because the answer is so simple. I just happened to want to draw chickens." (Her "chicken" book received the Caldecott Medal.)

Barbara Cooney's illustrations always contain many wonderful details, all of which are accurate. "If I put enough in my pictures," she says, "there will be something for everyone." She received a second Caldecott Medal for *Ox-Cart Man*, and a story she both wrote and illustrated, *Island Boy*, was a Boston Globe/Horn Book Honor Book.

Valentine for Earth

Oh, it will be fine
To rocket through space
And see the reverse
Of the moon's dark face,

To travel to Saturn
Or Venus or Mars,
Or maybe discover
Some uncharted stars.

But do they have anything
Better than we?
Do you think, for instance,
They have a blue sea

For sailing and swimming?
Do the planets have hills
With raspberry thickets
Where a song sparrow fills

The summer with music?
And do they have snow
To silver the roads
Where the school buses go?

Oh, I'm all for rockets
And worlds cold or hot,
But I'm wild in love
With the planet we've got!

FRANCES FROST

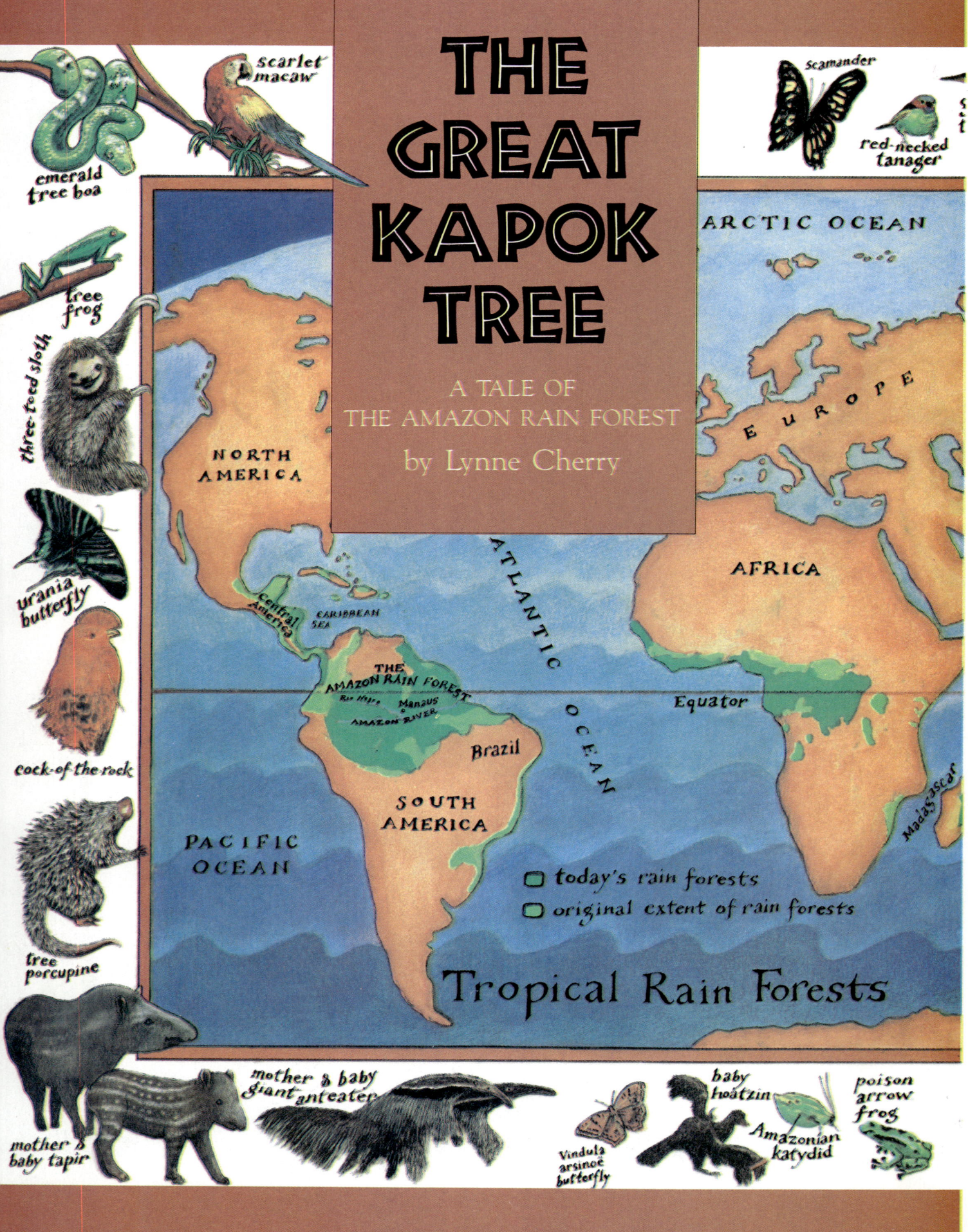

THE GREAT KAPOK TREE

A TALE OF THE AMAZON RAIN FOREST

by Lynne Cherry

golden tanager

parrot

squirrel monkey

jaguar

Anteos menippe butterfly

tamandua -or- anteater

boa constrictor

silky anteater

moustached tamarin

woolly monkey

iguana

Passion-flower butterfly

Siproeta stelenes butterfly

kinkajou

violet-tailed sylph

EMERGENTS

CANOPY

UNDERSTORY

Emergents

Canopy

Middle Layer

Shrub Layer

Herb Layer

ASIA

Japan

PACIFIC OCEAN

India

Indochina

Philippines

Malaysia

Indonesia

New Guinea

INDIAN OCEAN

AUSTRALIA

of the World

ANTARCTICA

chestnut-capped

puffbird

parakeet

blue morpho butterfly

ocelot

Hamadryas arinome butterfly

red-legged honey creeper

Papilio androgeus butterfly

In the Amazon rain forest it is always hot, and in that heat everything grows, and grows, and grows. The tops of the trees in the rain forest are called the canopy. The canopy is a sunny place that touches the sky. The animals that live there like lots of light. Colorful parrots fly from tree to tree. Monkeys leap from branch to branch. The bottom of the rain forest is called the understory. The animals that live in the understory like darkness. There, silent snakes curl around hanging vines. Graceful jaguars watch and wait.

And in this steamy environment the great Kapok tree shoots up through the forest and emerges above the canopy.

This is the story of a community of animals that live in one such tree in the rain forest.

Two men walked into the rain forest. Moments before, the forest had been alive with the sounds of squawking birds and howling monkeys. Now all was quiet as the creatures watched the two men and wondered why they had come.

The larger man stopped and pointed to a great Kapok tree. Then he left.

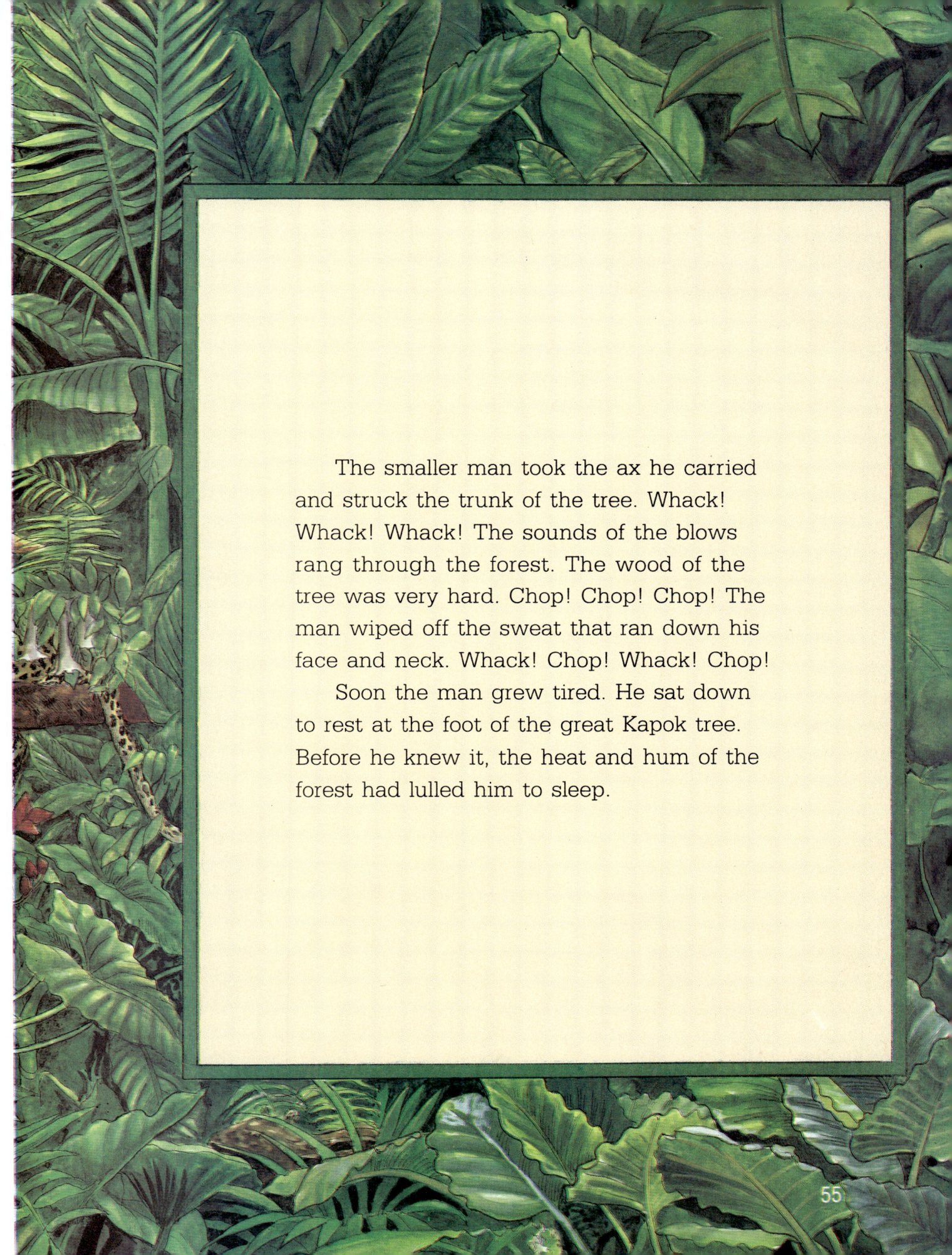

The smaller man took the ax he carried and struck the trunk of the tree. Whack! Whack! Whack! The sounds of the blows rang through the forest. The wood of the tree was very hard. Chop! Chop! Chop! The man wiped off the sweat that ran down his face and neck. Whack! Chop! Whack! Chop!

Soon the man grew tired. He sat down to rest at the foot of the great Kapok tree. Before he knew it, the heat and hum of the forest had lulled him to sleep.

A boa constrictor lived in the Kapok tree. He slithered down its trunk to where the man was sleeping. He looked at the gash the ax had made in the tree. Then the huge snake slid very close to the man and hissed in his ear: "Senhor, this tree is a tree of miracles. It is my home, where generations of my ancestors have lived. Do not chop it down."

A bee buzzed in the sleeping man's ear: "Senhor, my hive is in this Kapok tree, and I fly from tree to tree and flower to flower collecting pollen. In this way I pollinate the trees and flowers throughout the rain forest. You see, all living things depend on one another."

A troupe of monkeys scampered down from the canopy of the Kapok tree. They chattered to the sleeping man: "Senhor, we have seen the ways of man. You chop down one tree, then come back for another and another. The roots of these great trees will wither and die, and there will be nothing left to hold the earth in place. When the heavy rains come, the soil will be washed away and the forest will become a desert."

A toucan, a macaw, and a cock-of-the-rock flew down from the canopy. "Senhor!" squawked the toucan, "you must not cut down this tree. We have flown over the rain forest and seen what happens once you begin to chop down the trees. Many people settle on the land. They set fires to clear the underbrush, and soon the forest disappears. Where once there was life and beauty only black and smoldering ruins remain."

A bright and small tree frog crawled along the edge of a leaf. In a squeaky voice he piped in the man's ear: "Senhor, a ruined rain forest means ruined lives . . . many ruined lives. You will leave many of us homeless if you chop down this great Kapok tree."

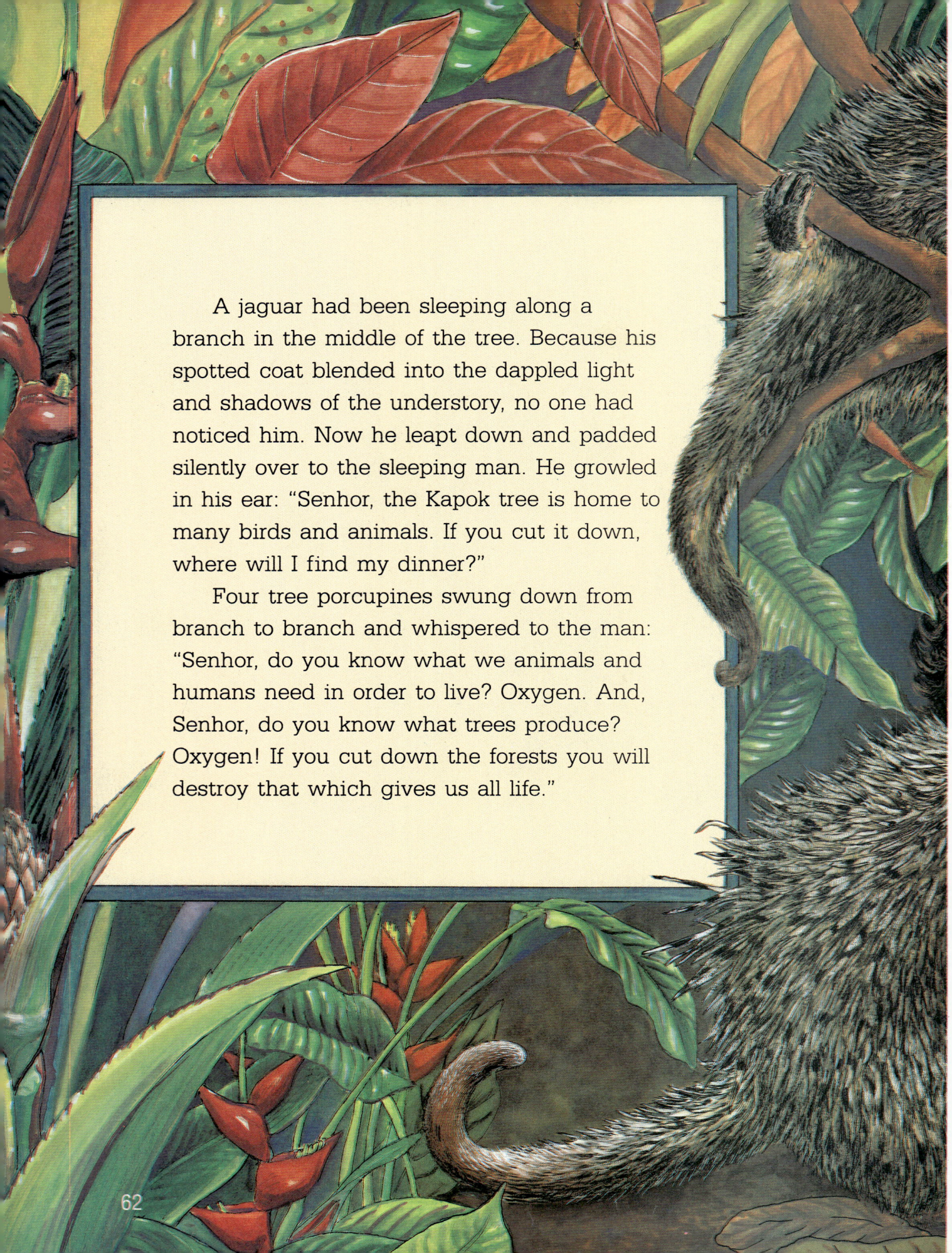

A jaguar had been sleeping along a branch in the middle of the tree. Because his spotted coat blended into the dappled light and shadows of the understory, no one had noticed him. Now he leapt down and padded silently over to the sleeping man. He growled in his ear: "Senhor, the Kapok tree is home to many birds and animals. If you cut it down, where will I find my dinner?"

Four tree porcupines swung down from branch to branch and whispered to the man: "Senhor, do you know what we animals and humans need in order to live? Oxygen. And, Senhor, do you know what trees produce? Oxygen! If you cut down the forests you will destroy that which gives us all life."

Several anteaters climbed down the Kapok tree with their young clinging to their backs. The unstriped anteater said to the sleeping man: "Senhor, you are chopping down this tree with no thought for the future. And surely you know that what happens tomorrow depends upon what you do today. The big man tells you to chop down a beautiful tree. He does not think of his own children, who tomorrow must live in a world without trees."

A three-toed sloth had begun climbing down from the canopy when the men first appeared. Only now did she reach the ground. Plodding ever so slowly over to the sleeping man, she spoke in her deep and lazy voice: "Senhor, how much is beauty worth? Can you live without it? If you destroy the beauty of the rain forest, on what would you feast your eyes?"

A child from the Yanomamo tribe who lived in the rain forest knelt over the sleeping man. He murmured in his ear: "Senhor, when you awake, please look upon us all with new eyes."

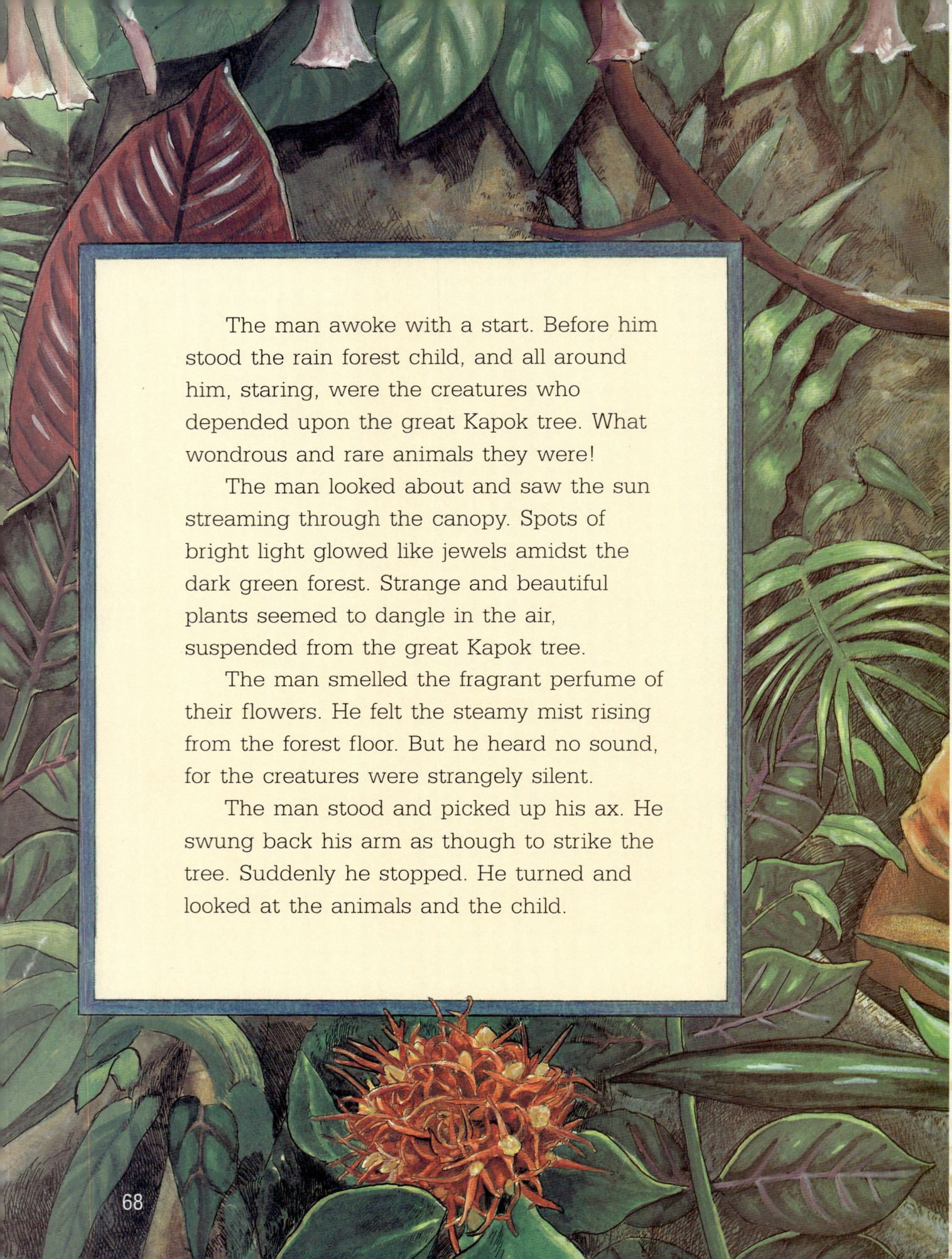

The man awoke with a start. Before him stood the rain forest child, and all around him, staring, were the creatures who depended upon the great Kapok tree. What wondrous and rare animals they were!

The man looked about and saw the sun streaming through the canopy. Spots of bright light glowed like jewels amidst the dark green forest. Strange and beautiful plants seemed to dangle in the air, suspended from the great Kapok tree.

The man smelled the fragrant perfume of their flowers. He felt the steamy mist rising from the forest floor. But he heard no sound, for the creatures were strangely silent.

The man stood and picked up his ax. He swung back his arm as though to strike the tree. Suddenly he stopped. He turned and looked at the animals and the child.

He hesitated. Then he dropped the ax and walked out of the rain forest.

Meet
LYNNE CHERRY

"Keep everything that you have written," Lynne Cherry advises children who want to become writers. Her old stories and drawings probably smell like chocolate. She kept them all in a chocolate box for many years.

When she was growing up in Pennsylvania, Cherry spent time in the woods watching animals and nature. She remembers seeing the trees and fields disappear as new houses and roads appeared. These experiences helped her write *The Great Kapok Tree,* which takes place in a rain forest.

Lynne Cherry wants to "try to make the world a better place." One way she helps is by donating her artwork to groups that work to save the Earth.

Why Save the Rain Forest?

Rain Forests Around the World
by Donald Silver

North America

Atlantic Ocean

Pacific Ocean

Africa

West Africa
- Covering about 64,000 square miles, this rain forest is home to colorful parrots and butterflies.
- Ninety percent of the forest that once was is now gone.

Caribbean Sea

Mexico, Central America, and the Caribbean
- The rain forests south of the United States are disappearing rapidly.
- Many migrating birds spend winters in these rain forests.
- Scientists have begun to study how to grow Central American rain-forest plants from seeds.

South America

Atlantic Ocean

Amazon Basin
- This is the largest rain forest in the world.
- It extends over nine South American countries and covers about 2.3 million square miles.
- It is rich in plant and animal life; new species are discovered every year.
- The world's second longest river, the Amazon, flows through this rain forest.

Central Africa
- The largest rain forest in Africa is located here.
- It is mostly unexplored.
- Thousands of its plant species are found nowhere else on Earth.

Rain forests cover 3.3 million square miles of our planet. That may sound like a lot but it is only six percent of the Earth's surface. Rain forests are disappearing fast.

Here is a map showing where the rain forests are located and a brief description of what makes some of them special:

Europe

Mediterranean Sea

Asia

Pacific Ocean

Philippines
- Thousands of kinds of plants and many beautiful and exotic birds fill 25,000 square miles of rain forest on the Philippine islands.

Southeast Asia
- Some countries here protect parts of their rain forests. Others do not, putting many plants and animals in danger of extinction.

New Guinea
- In these 270,000 square miles of rain forest, you can see a butterfly with a ten-inch wing span.

India
- Parts of the subcontinent's 78,000 square miles of rain forest have already been turned into national parks.

Indonesia
- More than 425,000 square miles of rain forest are spread over the islands that make up Indonesia.
- The world's biggest flower, the tallest flower, and about ten thousand kinds of trees grow here.

Australia

Madagascar
- The 14,000 square-mile rain forest on this island was twice as large just fifty years ago.
- It is the place to visit to see lemurs, a chameleon the size of your thumb, and thousands of orchids.

Australia
- Only about 4,000 square miles of rain forest grow on the island continent but they are still worth saving.

and my heart soars

The beauty of the trees,
the softness of the air,
the fragrance of the grass,
    speaks to me.

The summit of the mountain,
the thunder of the sky,
the rhythm of the sea,
    speaks to me.

The faintness of the stars,
the freshness of the morning,
the dew drop on the flower,
    speaks to me.

The strength of fire,
the taste of salmon,
the trail of the sun,
And the life that never goes away,
    They speak to me.

And my heart soars.

Chief Dan George

The British Columbia landscape surrounds Chief Dan George, a poet and member of the Salish nation.

In Memory

It took a wise man to dream big,
To dream great,
To talk of peace, brotherhood, and love
When all around was hate.
It took a strong man
To stand tall,
To speak of liberty and justice
And dignity for all.
He saw a great country
With some growing still to do.
He dreamed of a better world
Where freedom could ring true.
And so today we'll gather
For a birthday celebration
For a man who sought to change the mind
And heart of a nation.
Of liberty and brotherhood and peace
Today we'll sing
As we celebrate the memory of
Martin Luther King.

Ericka Northrop

THE STREETS ARE FREE

by Kurusa

illustrated by Sandra Speidel

Not very long ago, when Carlitos's grandfather was a boy, mountain lions roamed the hills of Venezuela. One particular mountain was covered with forests and bushes, small creeks and dirt paths. Every morning the mist would reach down and touch the flowers and the butterflies.

On the hill above the town of Caracas, where Cheo, Carlitos, and Camila now live, there was just one house. It was a simple house made of mud and dried leaves from sugar cane and banana plants. In the mornings, when the family went to fetch water, they often saw lion's tracks in the soft earth. Later, they would stop by the creeks to catch sardines for dinner.

Years passed and more people came from towns and villages all over Venezuela to make their homes on the mountainside.

They built their houses of wood and the children played among the trees, in the creeks and on the open fields.

The forest began to grow towards the new village, and the village began to grow towards the forest.

The dirt road that led to the big city was soon covered with asphalt.

And more people came.

There were so many houses that they reached right to the top of the mountain where the lion tracks used to be. The creeks became sewers. The dirt paths were littered with garbage. The mountain became a very poor town called the 'barrio' San José.

The children who used to play in the open fields could no longer play there, nor in the forest, nor in the streams.

The fields in the valleys were now filled with office towers. The whole mountain was covered with houses. The main road became a highway. There were only a few trees and not one flower. The children had nowhere to play.

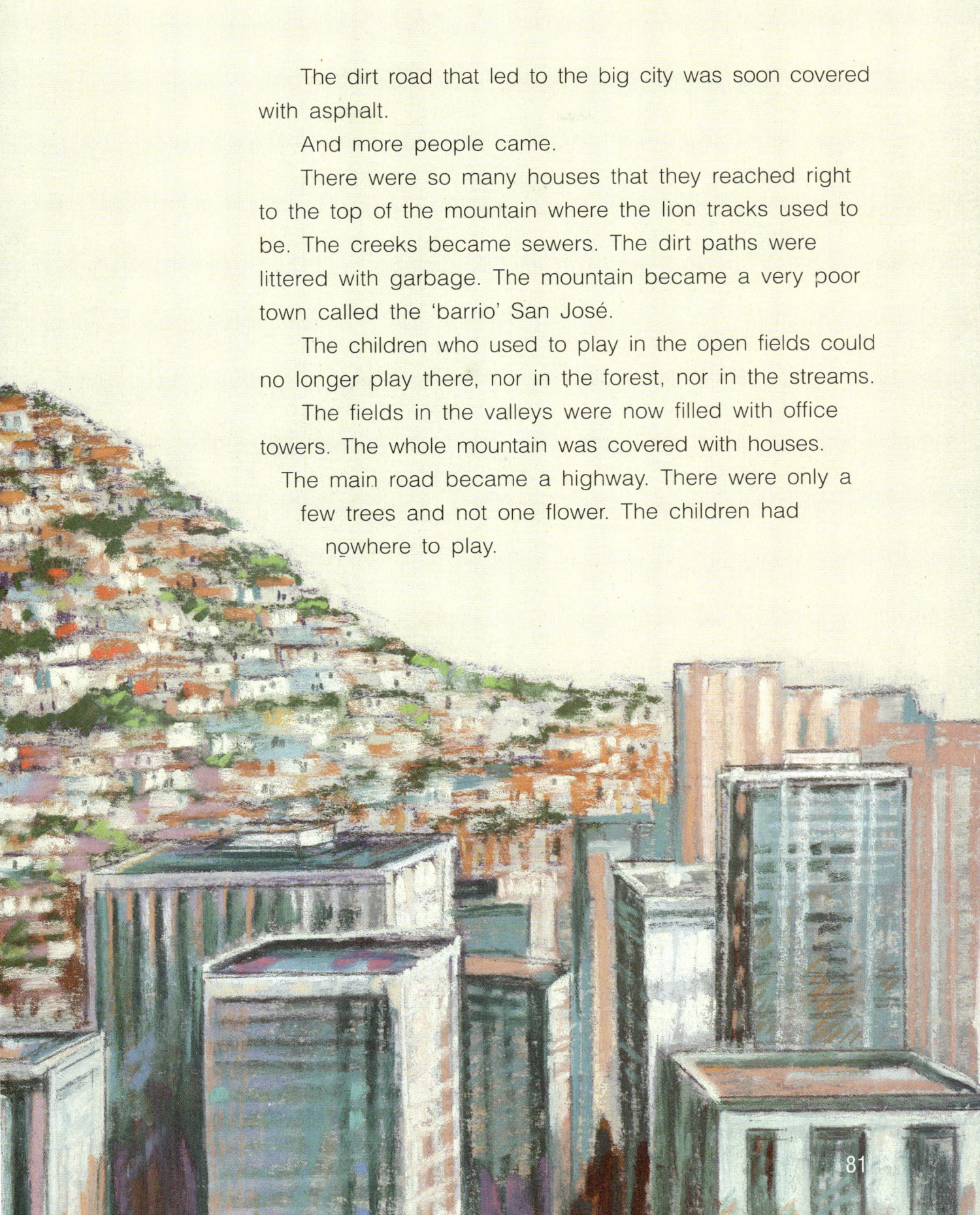

After school, Cheo, Carlitos, and Camila went to a house that was converted into a library. There they read books and played with clay and paints and board games and all kinds of interesting things. But they had nowhere to play hopscotch, or soccer, or baseball, or tag.

After they left the library, they played in the street.

One day, while they were playing leapfrog, a grocery truck came barrelling down the street. The driver shouted:

"Get out of the way! Let me through!"

"The streets are free," said the boys. But the truck was much bigger and more powerful than the children. So they walked to the top of the mountain to fly their kites. In about half an hour, every one of the kites was tangled in the hydro wires.

The children went back down the mountain to play ball. But the ball kept getting lost in people's washing and trapped on roof tops.

One woman ran out of her house when the children were trying to fetch the ball.

"Get out of here," she shouted, "or I'll hit you with my broom."

"The streets are free," said the youngest boy. But the children knew they had better leave her alone.

Dejected, they went to the library. They sat down on the steps and thought.

"There must be somewhere we can play," said Camila.

"Let's go see the mayor and tell him we need somewhere to play," suggested another.

SAN JOSÉ LIBRARY

83

"Where does he live?" asked Carlitos, the smallest boy. The children looked at each other. Nobody knew.

"Let's go to City Hall. That can't be too far away."

"But we can't go there without adults. They won't listen to us at City Hall," said Camila with big, sad eyes.

"Then let's ask our parents."

So the children went from house to house to ask their parents to go with them to City Hall. But their parents were cooking, sewing, washing, repairing, away working, in other words . . . busy.

The children returned to the library steps. They just sat there and felt very sad.

Then the librarian appeared.

"Why all the sad faces?" he asked.

The children told him.

"What do you want to tell the mayor?"

"We want a playground."

"Do you know where?"

"Yes," said Carlitos, "in an empty lot near the bottom of the mountain."

"Do you know what it should look like?"

"Well . . ."

"Why don't you come inside and discuss it?"

They talked for more than an hour. Cheo, the oldest boy, took notes on a large pad.

"Good," said the librarian, "and now what do you want to do?"

"We're still in the same boat," said Camila. "What good is a piece of paper if the adults don't go with us to see the mayor?"

"Won't they go with you?"

"They won't even listen to us," Camila said.

"Have you tried going alone?"

"Well, no."

"So, what do you want to do?"

The children looked at each other.

"Let's make a banner," said Cheo.

They all worked together and made a sign that said:

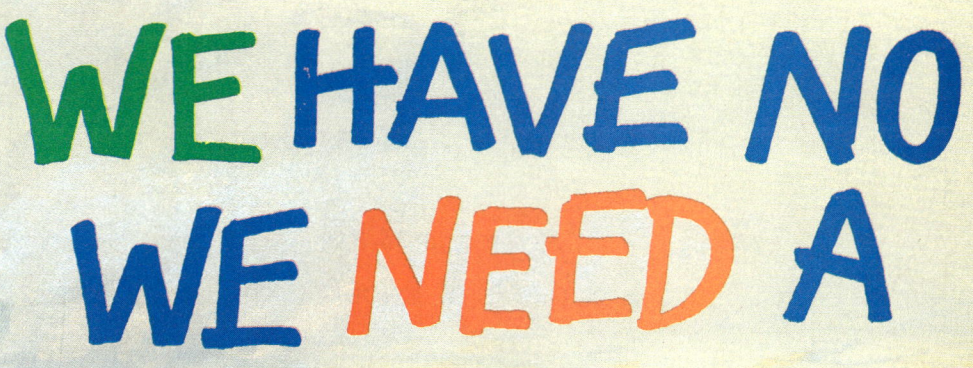

WE HAVE NO
WE NEED A

"Tomorrow we'll plan the details," said the librarian, and he left for the chess club.

The children put the finishing touches on their sign.

"It's perfect like this!"

They rolled up the sign and the large list with their notes.

"We're ready," they said.

Again the children looked at each other.

"Why don't we go right now?" a few children said at the same time.

With the banner and the large list of notes rolled up under their arms, the children of San José walked to City Hall.

86

WHERE TO PLAY PLAYGROUND

City Hall was even bigger than they imagined. The doorway was very high. Standing in the middle of it was a big, fat man.

"No one comes in here," he said.

"We came to ask for a playground."

"We came to see the people at City Hall. We need a playground."

"But the people at the Council don't want to see you. Go home or I'll call the police."

"Look, this is the kind of playground we want," said Carlitos, innocently, and he unrolled the paper with their notes on it.

Camila said, "We need somewhere to play," and she unrolled the banner.

"Get out of here!" shouted the fat man.

"The streets are free!" Cheo shouted back, and he sat down.

"We're not going to move until they listen to us," said another boy. "In the library they told us that City Hall is here to listen to us."

Back in San José, the mothers were worried. They couldn't find their children. Somebody said she saw them leaving the library with some big sheets of paper.

"Oh no," mumbled the librarian. "I think I know where they are."

The fat man in the doorway of City Hall was yelling so much his face was turning redder and redder. A crowd gathered around City Hall to see what all the fuss was about.

Then everything happened at once.

The mothers, the librarian, and the police all arrived at City Hall at the same time.

The mothers shouted, "What are you doing?"

"Take them away!" shouted the fat man to the police. "They're disturbing the peace." The policemen started pulling the children by their arms.

"Excuse me," the librarian raised one hand, "but what is going on here?"

"They won't let us talk to anyone about our playground," said Carlitos.

"The police are going to arrest them and put them in jail for their bad behaviour," said the fat man.

89

Then one mother who was even bigger and fatter than he stood in front of the children.

"Oh no, you don't," she said. "If you put a hand on these kids, you have to arrest me, too."

"And me, too," said another mother.

"And me," shouted the rest of the mothers.

Suddenly, standing in the doorway of City Hall, were the mayor, a reporter, and a municipal engineer.

"What's going on here?" the mayor asked.

"We need a playground."

"They want to arrest us."

"Those people are starting a riot."

They were all talking at once.

"Let the children speak," the librarian suggested.

"Yes, I'd like to talk to the children," said the reporter, getting out her notebook. They told her their story.

When they were finished, the mayor turned to the municipal engineer. "Is there space for them to have a playground?"

"Yes!" the children shouted together. "We know where. We can show you."

"Why don't you come and see it?" asked the librarian.

"Um—," said the engineer.

"Uhmmmmmmm—," said the mayor. "Tomorrow. Tomorrow we'll look at it. I don't have time now. I'm very busy. But tomorrow, tomorrow for sure. Ahem. Remember, we are here to serve you." Then the mayor shook hands with all the mothers.

"I knew it," said Camila.

"I would very much like to go with you," said the reporter. So the children, the mothers, the librarian, and the reporter all went to see the empty lot.

"What do you want the playground to look like?" the reporter asked. The children began to read their list. The reporter took lots of notes and wrote down everything on their sign:

We need a playground
   with trees
   and shrubs
   and flower seeds
    swings
   an old tractor to climb on
   and sticks to dig with
A house for dolls
   a lasso to play cowboys
Lots of room for baseball,
   volleyball and soccer,
   to have races and
    fly kites,
   to play leapfrog, tag,
   kick-the-can,
  blind man's bluff
   and hide and seek
  grass to roll on
   and do gymnastics
A patio to play on
   and a bench
  for our parents
    to sit and visit.

   THE END

The next day, the library was empty. The children sat on the steps.

"I think," sighed Camila, "I think that nothing's going to happen."

"What if we went to City Hall again with our big brothers and sisters?" asked Carlitos.

"They'll put us in jail," Camila said.

A week passed.

One day, the librarian appeared in the doorway smiling. He was holding a newspaper with a huge headline:

THE CHILDREN OF SAN JOSÉ
TAKE ON CITY HALL
They ask for special park
The mayor doesn't come through

"That's us!" said Cheo.

"We're famous!" laughed Carlitos.

"Yeah, but they're still not going to do anything," said Camila.

She was wrong. The same afternoon, the mayor, the municipal engineer and three assistants came to the barrio.

"We came to see the land for the playground. Soon we'll give it to you," they said proudly.

"Very soon," said the engineer.

"Very, very soon," smiled the mayor.

Then it happened: One morning, the assistants tied a red ribbon across the entrance to the empty lot. At twelve o'clock sharp, the mayor, dressed very elegantly and with freshly shined shoes, came and cut the ribbon with an extra-large pair of scissors.

"I get it," said Camila. "There's an election soon, isn't there? After the big ceremony, I bet nothing will happen."

This time Camila was right. Weeks passed and the engineers never came back. The empty lot that was supposed to be the playground was just collecting garbage. Little by little, the adults forgot about it. But the children didn't.

"What happened to our playground?" the children asked. The adults always gave the same answer:

"The politicians always promise but they never do anything."

Carlitos, Camila, and Cheo weren't satisfied. They sat on the edge of the mountain and looked down at the empty lot and thought about it all. Then Carlitos said:

"Why can't we have a playground anyway?"

"Are you crazy? It's very complicated."

"But if everybody helped, maybe . . . "

It was a crazy idea, but the young children started talking to their friends, who talked to their older brothers and sisters, who talked to their mothers, and the mothers talked to the fathers.

One day, Carlitos heard his uncle and some friends arguing about the playground. His uncle banged the

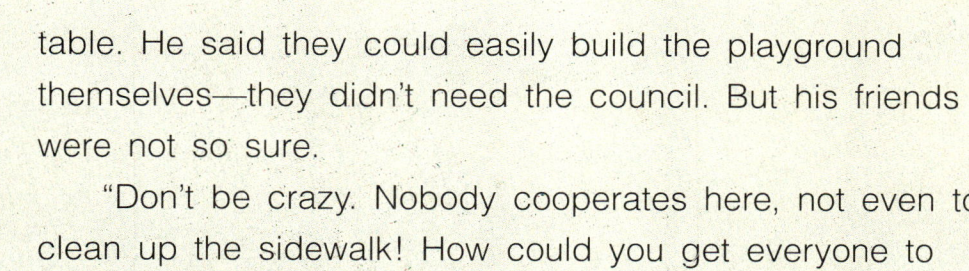

table. He said they could easily build the playground themselves—they didn't need the council. But his friends were not so sure.

"Don't be crazy. Nobody cooperates here, not even to clean up the sidewalk! How could you get everyone to build them a playground?"

"No, buddy, everyone knows each other. They'll help," said Carlitos's uncle.

"Forget it. You'll end up building it yourself."

"Alone? No. I'll help you," said one of the men.

"I will, too."

Time passed and more and more people talked about the idea. The neighbourhood committee organized a public meeting one Saturday. About fifty people came. The discussion lasted four hours and was very loud.

"We can't do it," said some.

"We can do it," said others.

There seemed no way to agree. Carlitos's uncle and the children passionately defended the idea, but most of the parents doubted it could be done without the politicians' help. After all the shouting, there was silence. It looked like the meeting was going to end that way until one mother remembered she had some planks of wood she didn't need. One father said he was a carpenter. One girl timidly said, "In my house we have some rope to make a swing with."

Everybody became very enthusiastic and suddenly they all had suggestions.

"I want to bring some nails," insisted one grandmother.

Carlitos, Cheo, and Camila all started jumping up and down.

"It's really going to happen!"

All the neighbours began to build the playground. They brought cement and bricks and buckets and sheets of aluminum and sandbags and old tires and wooden boards of every size.

They nailed and hammered and dug holes and planted and sanded. They all worked in their spare time.

99

On the wire fence the children put up a sign they made themselves:

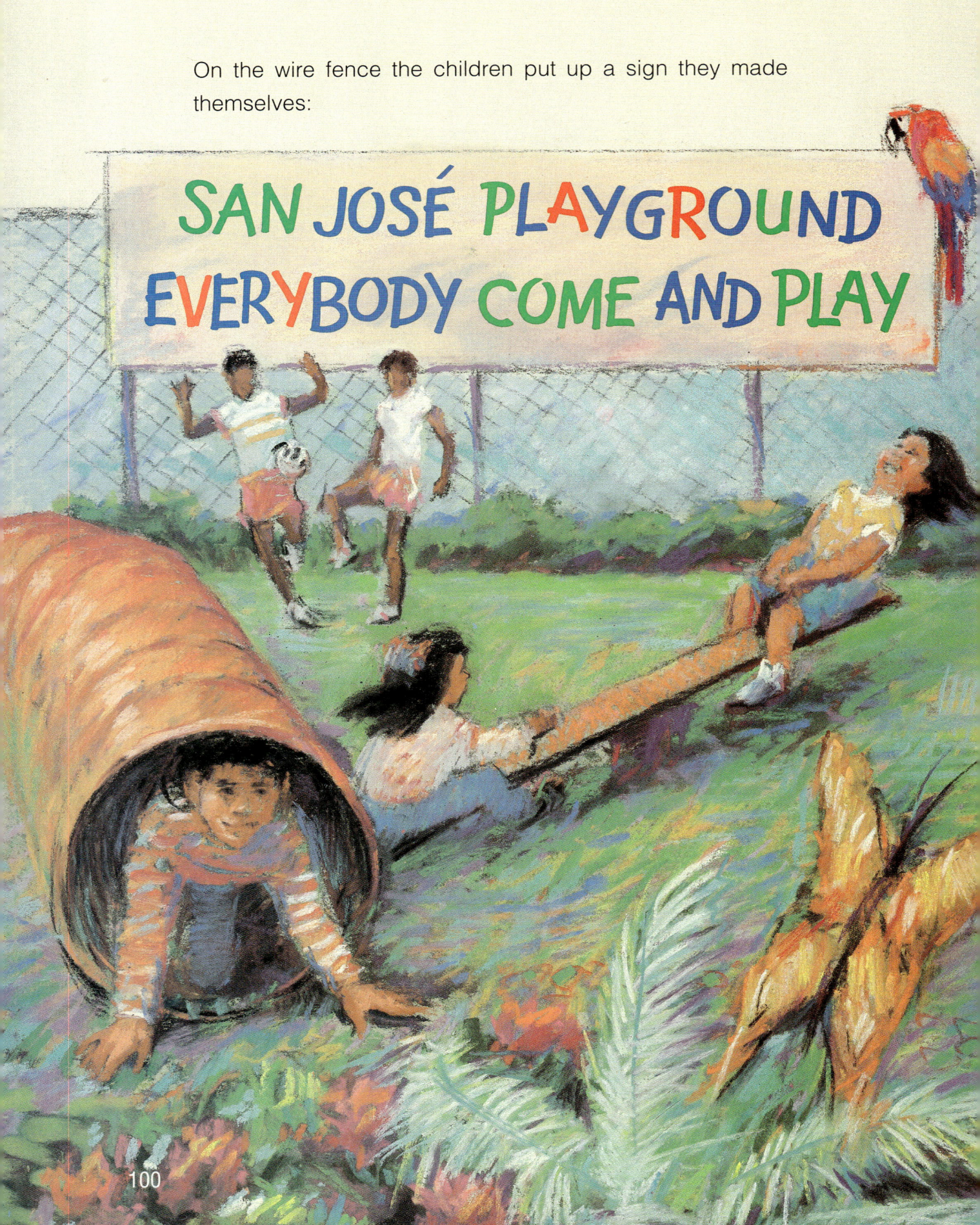

SAN JOSÉ PLAYGROUND
EVERYBODY COME AND PLAY

Meet Kurusa

Kurusa has spent over twelve years in her native Venezuela working with children in cultural and social programs. *The Streets Are Free* reflects some of her experiences with the children who use the public library in San José de La Urbina, a town on the edge of Caracas.

In her work promoting reading and children's literature in Venezuela, Kurusa has organized a bookmobile service and founded a publishing house for children's books.

The author lives in Caracas with her three children. She loves sailing and animals, and she has a sailboat with red sails on which a favorite seagull lives.

Preserven el Parque Elysian

by Mike Kellin

1. ¡Qué lin-do el par-que E-ly-sian! _____ ¡Qué lin-do el par-que E-ly-sian! _____ ¡Qué lin-do! (¡Qué lin-do!) ¡Qué lin-do! (¡Qué lin-do!) ¡Qué lin-do el par-que E-ly-sian! _____

1. ¡Qué lindo el parque Elysian!
2. ¡Me gusta el parque Elysian!

3. ¡El aire es libre, amigos!
4. ¡No queremos fincas en el parque!
5. ¡Queremos el zacate verde!
6. ¡El parque es suyo y mío!
7. ¡Los niños necesitan el parque!
8. ¡Preserven el parque Elysian!
9. ¡NO PASARÁN LOS BULLDOZERS!

1. Elysian Park is beautiful!
2. Elysian Park is my kind of park!

3. The air is free, my friends!
4. We don't want building in the park!
5. We want the green grass!
6. The park is yours and mine!
7. The children need the park!

8. Save Elysian Park!
9. STOP THE BULLDOZERS!

Illustration, by José Ortega, of musicians playing instruments commonly used in South America: bongo drums, a panpipe, and a charango.

Unit 2

Forces of Nature

Meet
Brenda Z. Guiberson

Brenda Guiberson got the idea for Cactus Hotel after several trips with her family to the Arizona desert. The sights and sounds of the desert thrilled her.

Guiberson enjoys researching and writing children's books. She says, "It's hard work but fun and surprises pop up all along the way."

Meet
Megan Lloyd

For Megan Lloyd, research is a very big part of her work. When she draws pictures for fiction stories, Lloyd uses costumes and lighting to explore the characters and setting. She says, "With nonfiction books, I carry my research even further, usually traveling to the geographical location in which the book is set."

Lloyd's research has taken her from the Saguaro National Monument in Tucson, Arizona (for Cactus Hotel) to a lobster boat off the coast of Maine!

CACTUS HOTEL

Written by Brenda Z. Guiberson

Illustrated by Megan Lloyd

On a hot, dry day in the desert, a bright-red fruit falls from a tall saguaro cactus. *Plop*. It splits apart on the sandy floor. Two thousand black seeds glisten in the sunlight.

When the air cools in the evening, an old pack rat comes out and eats the juicy fruit. Then he skitters across the sand. A seed left clinging to his whiskers falls off under a paloverde tree.

It is a good place for the seed to drop. A spotted ground squirrel looking for something to eat does not see it. A house finch chirping high in the paloverde does not see it.

After many dry days, a heavy rain falls on the desert. Soon a young cactus sprouts up from the ground.

Slowly, slowly the seedling grows. The paloverde protects it from the hot summer sun and cold winter nights. After ten years the cactus is only four inches high. It is just big enough for desert ants to climb its spiny sides.

After a rainstorm, when the desert blooms with color, the cactus pulls in water with its long roots and looks fat. A young pack rat stops to drink the water that drips off the tree. Then she scurries off, looking for a dry place to make a nest.

When there is no rain, the cactus uses up the water it has stored inside and looks thin. The paloverde loses its tiny leaves. But there is always some shade for the cactus below. After twenty-five years, the cactus is two feet tall. A jackrabbit cools off beside it and gnaws on the green pulp. But when a coyote moves in the distance, the jackrabbit disappears into a nearby hole.

After fifty years the cactus stands ten feet tall and looks straight and strong beside the old paloverde. For the very first time, brilliant white-and-yellow flowers appear at the top of the cactus. Every spring from now on, the flowers will open for one night only and then close in the heat of the day. They beckon like a welcoming signal across the desert. At different times of the day and night birds, bees, and bats come for the nectar.

The flowers dry up, and after a month the bright-red fruit filled with black seeds is ripe and ready. A Gila woodpecker comes to eat. He looks around the cactus and decides to stay.

He has found the perfect place in the desert to begin a new hotel.

The woodpecker goes right to work, and the only tool
he uses is his long, hard beak. *Tap, tap, tap.* He bores into
the flesh of the cactus. *Tap, tap, tap.* He digs deep inside,
to make a space that is comfortable and roomy.

The cactus is not harmed. It forms a tough scab all
around the hole to protect itself from drying out. The
woodpecker gets a weatherproof nest that is shady on hot
days, and warm and insulated on frosty nights. And the
cactus gets something in return: The woodpecker likes to
eat the insects that can bring disease to the cactus.

After sixty years the cactus hotel is eighteen feet tall. To add more space, it begins to grow an arm. A woodpecker has a new hole in the trunk. Farther up, a white-winged dove makes a nest on the arm. And down below, an old hole is discovered by an elf owl. The birds feel safe, living high up in a prickly plant where nothing can reach them.

All around the desert there are holes of every size, for
ants and mice, lizards and snakes, rabbits and foxes. After
a hundred and fifty years, there are holes of every size
in the cactus, too. The giant plant has finally stopped
growing. It is fifty feet tall, with seven long branches.
It weighs eight tons—about as much as five automobiles.

Everybody wants to live in
the cactus hotel. Birds lay eggs
and pack rats raise their young.
Even insects and bats live there.

When one animal moves out,
another moves in. And every spring
they come for a special treat of nectar
and juicy red fruit.

Finally, after two hundred years, the old cactus sways
in a gust of wind and falls with a thud to the sandy floor.
Its great thorny arms crumble in the crash.

The creatures that lived up high must find other
homes. But those that prefer to live down low move right
in. A millipede, a scorpion, and many ants and termites
quickly find homes in the toppled hotel.

After many months, all that remains are the wooden
ribs that supported the cactus while it stood so tall. A
collared lizard dashes over the top, looking for insects.
A ground snake huddles in the shade below.

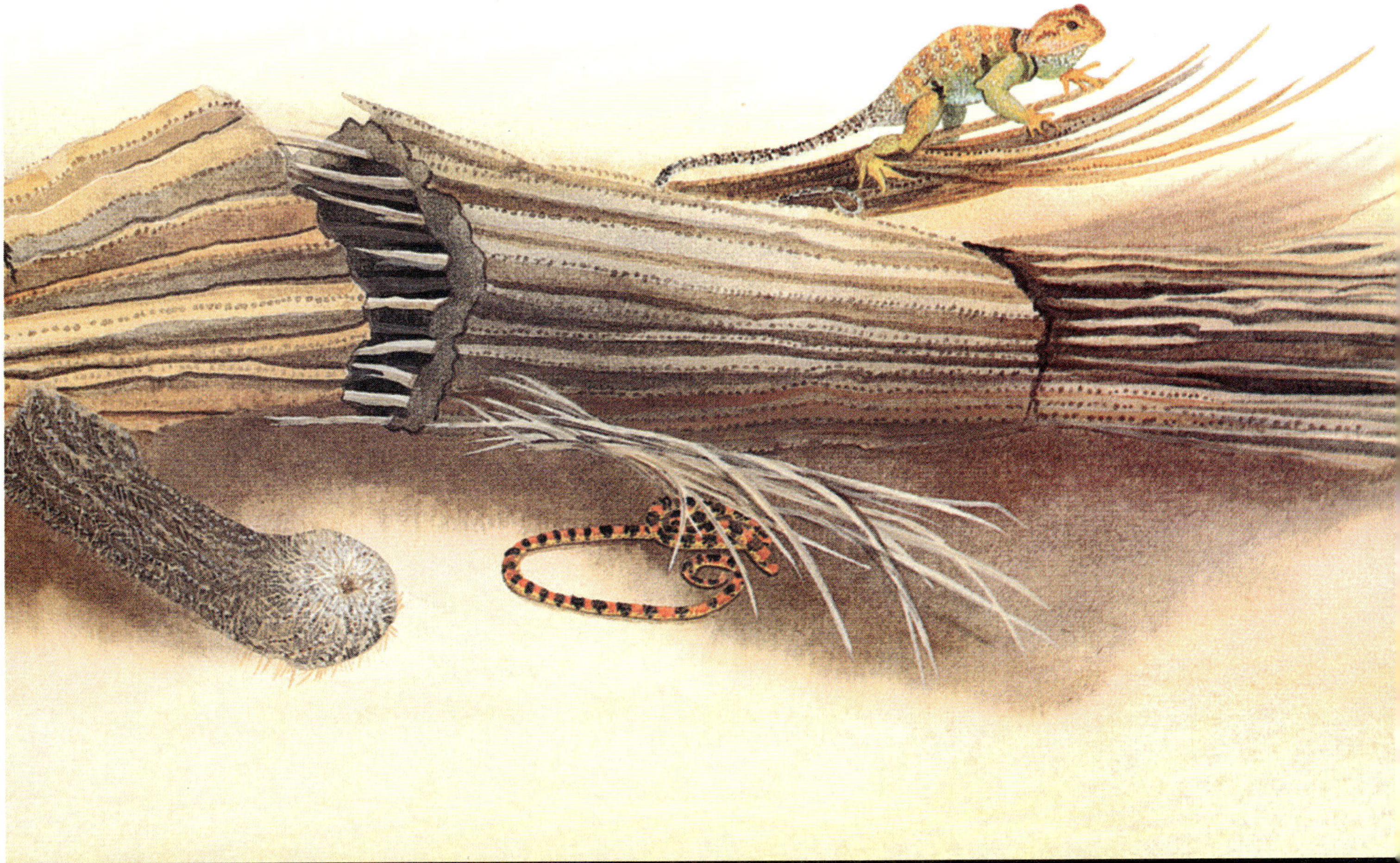

And all around, there is a forest of cacti slowly, slowly growing in the desert. Through hot and cold, wet and dry, some will survive long enough to become other cactus hotels.

An Incredible

As a liquid, gas, or solid, powered by the sun and the force of gravity, water travels over, under, and above the surface of Earth in an incredible journey called the water cycle.

PLAYERS: one to four, shrunk to the size of water molecules.

GOAL: First player to visit and write down all nine places and return to clouds wins! If playing alone, set timer and visit as many places as you can in one minute.

YOU NEED: scissors, paper, pencil, paper sack, playing pieces (pebbles, buttons, or seeds), "An Incredible Journey" playing board.

BEFORE PLAYING: Cut paper into six squares, number, and place in sack.

HERE'S HOW TO PLAY:

★ Place playing pieces on clouds to start.

★ Have first player draw number, read directions by clouds and move to next location. Example: if you draw "2," move to "glacier."

★ On a notepad, write or draw "glacier."

★ Return the number to bag, give to next player.

★ When your notepad shows all nine places, keep playing until you return to clouds.

★ Ready, Set, Evaporate! Condense! Melt! Freeze!

transpire — water leaving a plant as vapor

evaporate — changing from a liquid to a vapor or gas

Clouds

1	Condense and fall on soil
2	Condense and fall as snow on glacier
3	Condense and fall into lake
4/5	Condense and fall into ocean
6	Remain as part of water drop, stay in cloud

Ocean

| 1 2 | Evaporate and move into clouds |
| 3 4 5 6 | Remain in ocean |

Plant

| 1 2 3 4 | Evaporate (transpire) from plant and move into cloud |
| 5 6 | Remain within plant |

Lake

1	Filter into soil and into ground water
2	Drunk by animal
3	Flow into river
4	Evaporate and move into clouds
5 6	Remain in lake

Soil

1	Absorbed by roots of plants
2	Drain into river
3	Filter through soil into ground water
4 5	Evaporate and move into clouds
6	Remain in puddle on soil surface

Journey

FALCON
MAGAZINE KIDS
our wet world

Glacier

1. Melt and filter into ground water
2. Evaporate and move into clouds
3. Melt and flow into river
4.–8. Remain frozen in glacier

Animal

1.–2. As waste products, move into soil
3.–5. Evaporate and move into clouds
6. Stay within animal

River

1. Flow into lake
2. Filter into soil and into ground water
3. Flow into ocean
4. Drunk by animal
5. Evaporate and move into clouds
6. Remain in river

Ground Water

1. Filter into river
2.–3. Filter into lake
4.–6. Remain in ground water

Spring Rain

The storm came up so very quick
    It couldn't have been quicker.
I should have brought my hat along,
    I should have brought my slicker.

My hair is wet, my feet are wet,
    I couldn't be much wetter.
I fell into a river once
    But this is even better.

Marchette Chute

¡Que llueva!

¡Que llueva! ¡Que llueva!
la virgen de la cueva,
los pajaritos cantan,
las nubes se levantan,

¡Que si! ¡Que no!
¡Que caiga el chaparrón!

It's Raining!

It's raining! It's raining!
The cavern maiden's calling.
The little birds are singing,
All the clouds are lifting.

Oh yes—Oh no!
Oh! Let the downpour fall.

a traditional Puerto Rican song
English lyrics by Elena Paz

131

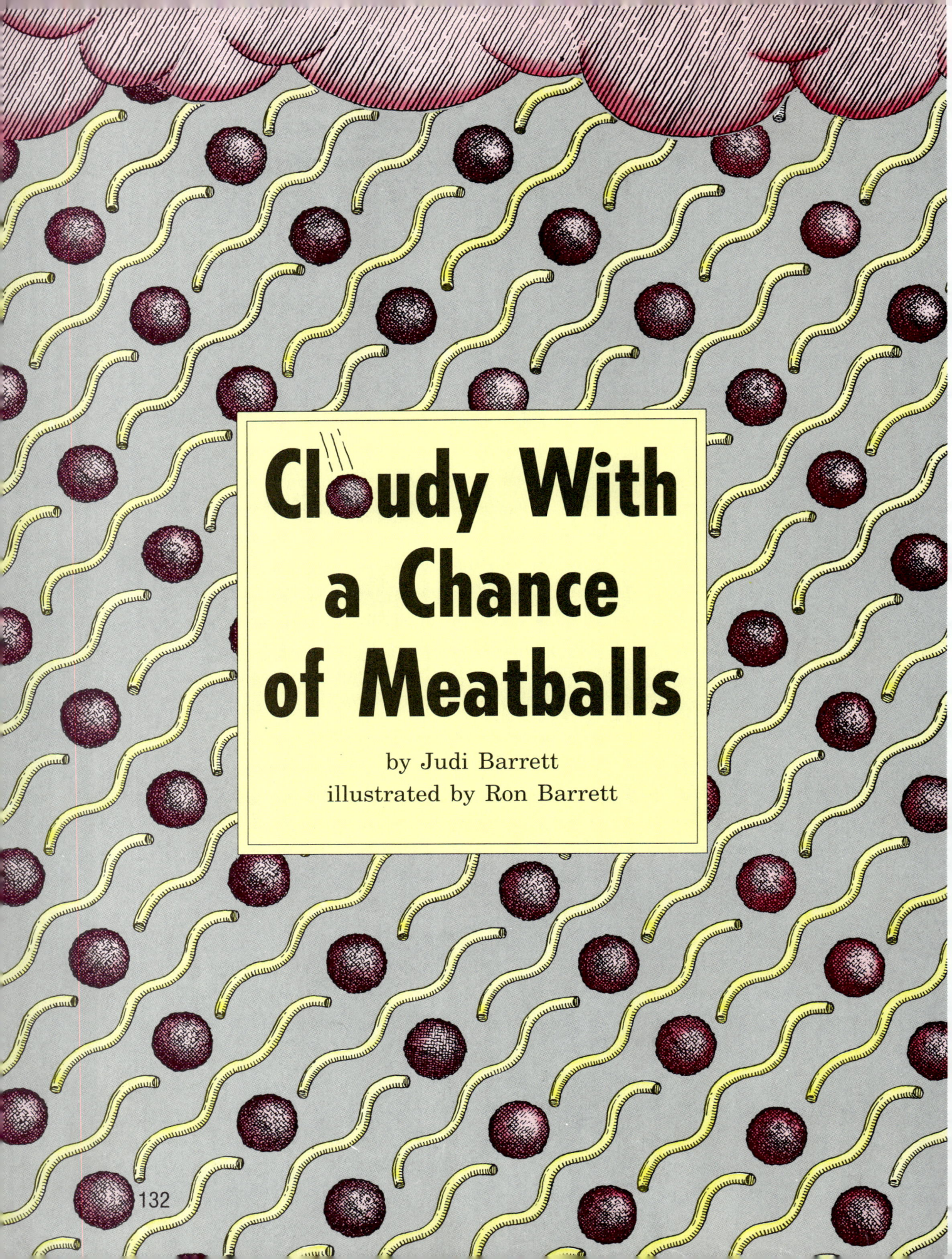

Cloudy With a Chance of Meatballs

by Judi Barrett

illustrated by Ron Barrett

We were all sitting around the big kitchen table. It was Saturday morning. Pancake morning. Mom was squeezing oranges for juice. Henry and I were betting on how many pancakes we each could eat. And Grandpa was doing the flipping.

Seconds later, something flew through the air headed toward the kitchen ceiling . . .

... and landed right on Henry.

After we realized that the flying object was only a pancake, we all laughed, even Grandpa. Breakfast continued quite uneventfully. All the other pancakes landed in the pan. And all of them were eaten, even the one that landed on Henry.

That night, touched off by the pancake incident at breakfast, Grandpa told us the best tall-tale bedtime story he'd ever told.

"Across an ocean, over lots of huge bumpy mountains, across three hot deserts, and one smaller ocean . . .

. . . there lay the tiny town of Chewandswallow.

In most ways, it was very much like any other tiny town. It had a Main Street lined with stores, houses with trees and gardens around them, a schoolhouse, about three hundred people, and some assorted cats and dogs.

But there were no food stores in the town of Chewandswallow. They didn't need any. The sky supplied all the food they could possibly want.

The only thing that was really different about Chewandswallow was its weather. It came three times a day, at breakfast, lunch, and dinner. Everything that everyone ate came from the sky.

Whatever the weather served, that was what they ate.

But it never rained rain. It never snowed snow. And it never blew just wind. It rained things like soup and juice. It snowed mashed potatoes and green peas. And sometimes the wind blew in storms of hamburgers.

141

The people could watch the weather report on television in the morning and they would even hear a prediction for the next day's food.

When the townspeople went outside, they carried their plates, cups, glasses, forks, spoons, knives, and napkins with them. That way they would always be prepared for any kind of weather.

If there were leftovers, and there usually were, the people took them home and put them in their refrigerators in case they got hungry between meals.

The menu varied.

By the time they woke up in the morning, breakfast was coming down.

After a brief shower of orange juice, low clouds of sunny-side-up eggs moved in followed by pieces of toast.

Butter and jelly sprinkled down for the toast. And most of the time it rained milk afterwards.

For lunch one day, frankfurters, already in their rolls, blew in from the northwest at about five miles an hour.

There were mustard clouds nearby. Then the wind shifted to the east and brought in baked beans.

A drizzle of soda finished off the meal.

Dinner one night consisted of lamb chops, becoming heavy at times, with occasional ketchup. Periods of peas and baked potatoes were followed by gradual clearing, with a wonderful Jell-O setting in the west.

The Sanitation Department of Chewandswallow had a rather unusual job for a sanitation department. It had to remove the food that fell on the houses and sidewalks and lawns. The workers cleaned things up after every meal and fed all the dogs and cats. Then they emptied some of it into the surrounding oceans for the fish and turtles and whales to eat. The rest of the food was put back into the earth so that the soil would be richer for the people's flower gardens.

Life for the townspeople was delicious until the weather took a turn for the worse.

One day there was nothing but Gorgonzola cheese all day long.

The next day there was only broccoli, all overcooked.

And the next day there were Brussels sprouts and peanut butter with mayonnaise.

Another day there was a pea soup fog. No one could see where they were going and they could barely find the rest of the meal that got stuck in the fog.

The food was getting larger and larger, and so were the portions. The people were getting frightened. Violent storms blew up frequently. Awful things were happening.

One Tuesday there was a hurricane of bread and rolls all day long and into the night. There were soft rolls and hard rolls, some with seeds and some without. There was white bread and rye and whole wheat toast. Most of it was larger than they had ever seen bread and rolls before. It was a terrible day. Everyone had to stay indoors. Roofs were damaged, and the Sanitation Department was beside itself. The mess took the workers four days to clean up, and the sea was full of floating rolls.

To help out, the people piled up as much bread as they could in their backyards. The birds picked at it a bit, but it just stayed there and got staler and staler.

There was a storm of pancakes one morning and a downpour of maple syrup that nearly flooded the town. A huge pancake covered the school. No one could get it off because of its weight, so they had to close the school.

Lunch one day brought fifteen-inch drifts of cream cheese and jelly sandwiches. Everyone ate themselves sick and the day ended with a stomachache.

There was an awful salt and pepper wind accompanied by an even worse tomato tornado. People were sneezing themselves silly and running to avoid the tomatoes. The town was a mess. There were seeds and pulp everywhere.

The Sanitation Department gave up. The job was too big.

Everyone feared for their lives. They couldn't go outside most of the time. Many houses had been badly damaged by giant meatballs, stores were boarded up and there was no more school for the children.

So a decision was made to abandon the town of Chewandswallow.
It was a matter of survival.

The people glued together the giant pieces of stale bread
sandwich-style with peanut butter . . .

. . . took the absolute necessities with them, and set sail on their rafts for a new land.

After being afloat for a week, they finally reached a small coastal town, which welcomed them. The bread had held up surprisingly well, well enough for them to build temporary houses for themselves out of it.

The children began school again, and the adults all tried to find places for themselves in the new land. The biggest change they had to make was getting used to buying food at a supermarket. They found it odd that the food was kept on shelves, packaged in boxes, cans and bottles. Meat that had to be cooked was kept in large refrigerators. Nothing came down from the sky except rain and snow. The clouds above their heads were not made of fried eggs. No one ever got hit by a hamburger again.

And nobody dared to go back to Chewandswallow to find out what had happened to it. They were too afraid."

Henry and I were awake until the very end of Grandpa's story. I remember his good-night kiss.

The next morning we woke up to see snow falling outside our window.

We ran downstairs for breakfast and ate it a little faster than usual so we could go sledding with Grandpa.

It's funny, but even as we were sliding down the hill we thought we saw a giant pat of butter at the top, and we could almost smell mashed potatoes.

Meet Judi Barrett

Judi Barrett has always had lots of imagination. When she was a child, she loved to make things. She made little people out of peanuts, horses out of pipe cleaners, and dolls out of old quilts.

As an adult, she has used her imagination for writing books, such as *Animals Should Definitely Not Wear Clothing, Benjamin's 365 Birthdays,* and *Cloudy With a Chance of Meatballs.*

Judi Barrett also gets very involved in the art for her books. "I see my books visually while I write them," she says. "The words come along with images of what the book should look like, the feeling it should have."

Meet Ron Barrett

What made Ron Barrett want to draw? It was those silly little characters in the comic books his father used to leave on the table. Ron Barrett remembers all the characters who lived "stacked up in the little boxes on the funny pages."

Ron has kept his sense of humor. Here is what he says about his pictures for *Cloudy With a Chance of Meatballs*: "The book took one year to design and draw. I used a very small pen. Hamburgers and pancakes actually posed for the pictures. I ate my models."

The Rains in Little Dribbles

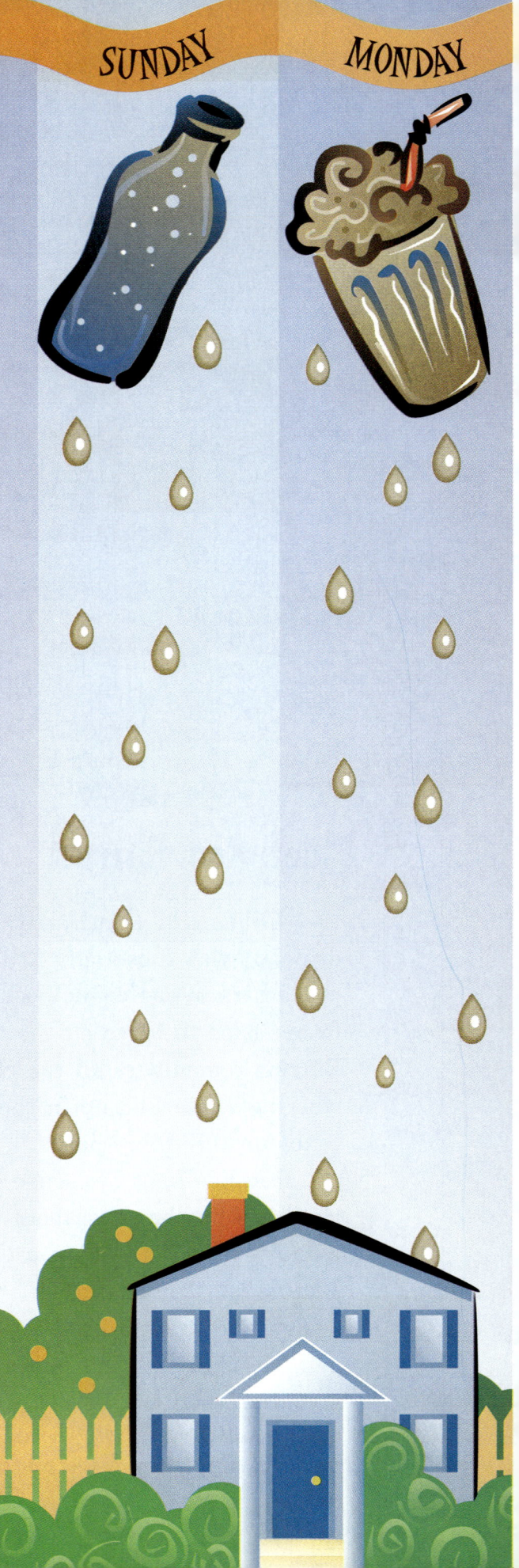

The rains in Little Dribbles
are the sort one rarely sees,
every Thursday it pours cola,
Friday showers herbal teas,
early Saturday a sprinkle
of sweet cider fills the air,
then on Sunday sarsaparilla
soaks the citizenry there.

Monday morning, mocha malteds
softly saturate the town,
while on Tuesday lemon droplets
drizzle delicately down,
but the rain that rains on Wednesday
is a watermelon tide,
so the folks in Little Dribbles
spend their Wednesdays safe inside.

Jack Prelutsky

158

WEATHER REPORT

Pointer in hand,
the weatherman stands
before the map.
"Here," he says,
tracking a thunderstorm.
"There," he says,
predicting fog.
"Forty percent,"
figuring snow squalls.
"A low, a high . . ."

But above us, the sky,
with a logic all its own
announces sun.

JANE YOLEN

TORNADO

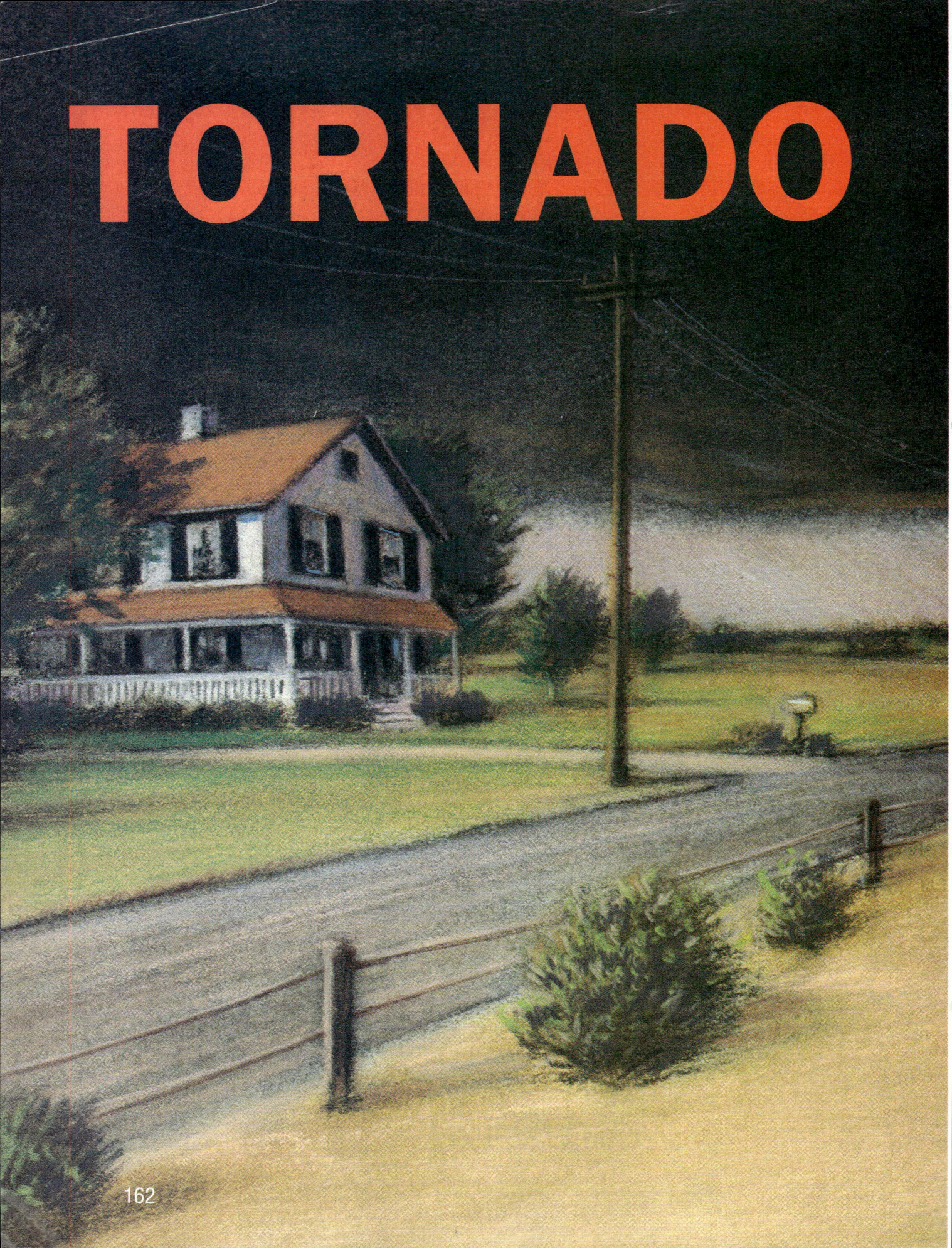

ALERT

by Franklyn M. Branley
illustrated by Paul Selwyn

Tornadoes are powerful storms.

On a tornado day the air is hot and still. Clouds build up rapidly. They get thick and dark. In the distance there is thunder and lightning, rain and hail.

Here and there parts of the clouds seem to reach toward the ground. Should these parts grow larger and become funnel shaped, watch out. The funnels could become tornadoes.

The funnel of a tornado is usually dark gray or black. It may also be yellowish or red.

The colors come from red and yellow dirt picked up by the tornado as it moves along the ground.

Tornadoes can strike most anywhere, but usually they happen where there is a lot of flat land. Most tornadoes occur in Texas, Oklahoma, Kansas, Nebraska, Iowa, and Missouri. Florida also has a lot of tornadoes.

Tornadoes can touch down over seas and lakes. When that happens, they are called waterspouts.

Most tornadoes occur during April, May, and June. That's when cold air meets warm air near the Earth's surface. The cold air pushes under the warm air. The warm air is lighter than the cold air and rises rapidly.

As the warm air moves upward, it spins around, or twists. That's why tornadoes are sometimes called twisters. Some people call them cyclones. The wind speed around the funnel of the tornado may reach 300 miles an hour. No other wind on Earth blows that fast.

As the hot air rises, it also spreads out. It makes a funnel of air, with the small part of the funnel touching the ground and the large part in the dark clouds. Air all around the tornado moves in toward the funnel. At the same time, storm winds push the twisting funnel, moving it along the Earth.

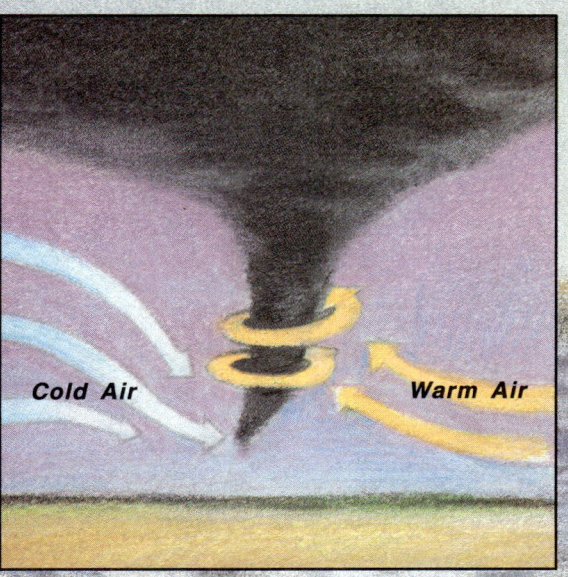

Cold Air   Warm Air

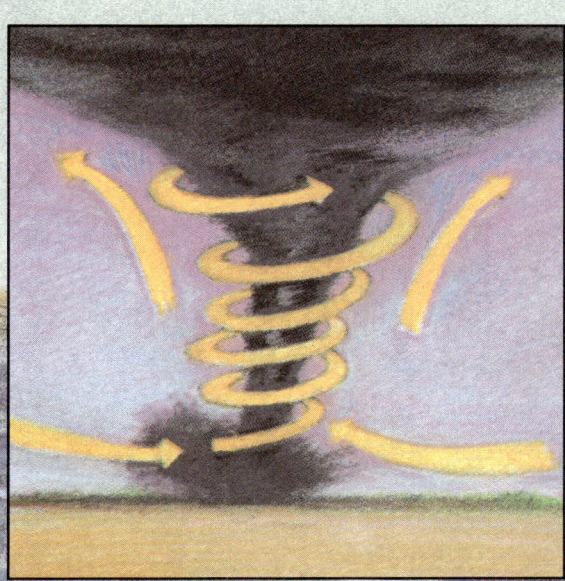

During tornado season in the United States, there may be 40 or 50 tornadoes in one week. Sometimes there are many more. Most are small. Usually a tornado blows itself out in less than an hour. Some last only a few seconds.

Small tornadoes don't travel far, and they cause little damage. Big tornadoes destroy everything in their paths. They may travel 200 miles and last several hours.

During a tornado there is thunder and lightning, rain and hail. And there is lots of noise. It can sound as loud as a freight train or a jet engine. The word *tornado* comes from a Latin word that means thunder. Some of the noise does come from thunder, but most of it comes from the roaring wind. There is lots of noise, and lots and lots of wind.

Tornadoes are very powerful, and some cause a lot of damage. Tornadoes can pick up branches and boards, stones and bricks, cars, and sometimes even people.

They can rip off roofs and leave a trail of wrecked houses. A tornado's path may be only 20 or 30 feet wide. Or it might be 1,000 feet or more—maybe even a mile.

In 1931 a tornado in Minnesota lifted a train off its tracks. The train and its passengers were carried through the air and dropped 80 feet from the tracks. There were 170 people on board. Though many people were hurt, only one person was killed. But in 1974 a series of tornadoes in Missouri, Illinois, Indiana, and 10 other states killed 315 people in 24 hours.

Scientists keep a close watch during tornado season. They use satellites that see storms developing. And there is radar to detect tornadoes.

Tornado spotters are people who watch for tornadoes. They tell radio and television stations to warn people about tornadoes while the twisters are still far away. The warnings tell people to go to a safe spot, where the tornado can't hurt them.

If a tornado is on its way, here's what you should do. Go to a nearby storm cellar. Storm cellars are underground rooms with heavy doors. They are safe.

If you are in a mobile home, get out of it. A tornado can rip apart a mobile home, even when it is tied down with strong cables. Lie face down in a ditch and cover your head with your hands. When you're in a ditch, sticks and stones flying through the air can't hit you.

If you are in a house, go to the basement and crouch under the stairs or under a heavy workbench. Or go to a closet that is far from an outside wall. Be sure to keep far away from windows. The wind could smash them and send splinters of glass through the air.

If you are in school, follow directions. Your teacher will take you to a basement or to an inside hall. Crouch on your knees near an inner wall. Bend over and clasp your hands behind your head. Most important, keep away from glass windows.

If you are out in the country in a car, don't try to race the tornado. Get out, and find a ditch to lie in.

When there's a tornado, there is also thunder and lightning. So keep away from metal things and from anything that uses electricity. Lightning can travel along metal pipes, and also along electric and telephone wires.

Listen to a battery radio. The radio will tell you when the storm has passed by. Stay where you are safe until you are sure the tornado is over.

Tornadoes are scary. Even if you are not right in the funnel, there is heavy rain all around, dark skies, thunder, lightning, and lots of wind. Often there will be hailstones. They may be as big as golf balls, or even bigger.

Don't panic. Know what to do when there is a tornado. And know where to go.

There is no way to stop tornadoes. But you can be safe from them when you know what to do.

Tornado Rules

- Don't panic.
- Listen.
- Look.
- Follow Directions.

172

MEET
FRANKLYN M. BRANLEY

When Franklyn Branley began to teach grade school, he noticed that there were not very many good science books for children. He decided to write some himself. He began the *Let's-Read-and-Find-Out* series and wrote more than thirty books for it about the moon, the stars, rockets, and many other science topics.

Branley wrote *Tornado Alert* for a specific reason. "It's important that everyone knows there are such things as tornadoes and that people can protect themselves." Some people have said that his books are too scary, but Branley believes they give information children need to know.

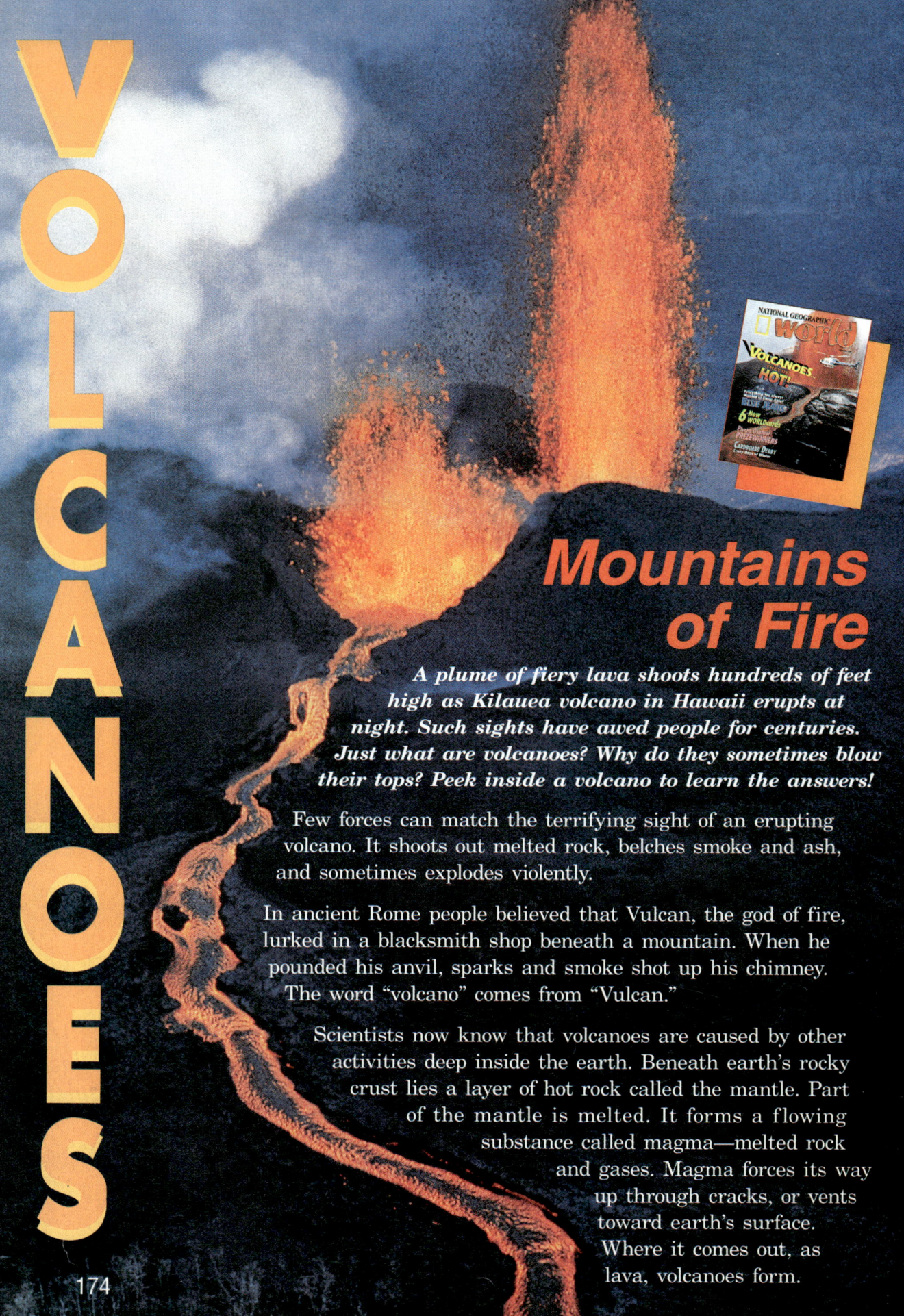

VOLCANOES

Mountains of Fire

A plume of fiery lava shoots hundreds of feet high as Kilauea volcano in Hawaii erupts at night. Such sights have awed people for centuries. Just what are volcanoes? Why do they sometimes blow their tops? Peek inside a volcano to learn the answers!

Few forces can match the terrifying sight of an erupting volcano. It shoots out melted rock, belches smoke and ash, and sometimes explodes violently.

In ancient Rome people believed that Vulcan, the god of fire, lurked in a blacksmith shop beneath a mountain. When he pounded his anvil, sparks and smoke shot up his chimney. The word "volcano" comes from "Vulcan."

Scientists now know that volcanoes are caused by other activities deep inside the earth. Beneath earth's rocky crust lies a layer of hot rock called the mantle. Part of the mantle is melted. It forms a flowing substance called magma—melted rock and gases. Magma forces its way up through cracks, or vents toward earth's surface. Where it comes out, as lava, volcanoes form.

Ash and steam roar from Augustine Volcano in Alaska. Such an explosive eruption can send ash miles high, darkening the sky for days.

Not all volcanoes look alike or behave the same. They differ in their shape and in how they erupt.

Some volcanoes, like Kilauea (kee-lau-AY-uh) in Hawaii, look like low hills. They send out thin, fluid lava that builds up in smooth layers. Gases in this lava escape easily, so eruptions are not usually noisy or dangerously explosive.

Other volcanoes, such as Mount St. Helens in Washington, are cone-shaped mountains that can erupt violently. Their lava is thick and pasty. As the magma rises to the surface, the gases, which cannot escape easily, expand and then explode. The volcano throws out ash and fragments of molten lava and rock. A third kind of volcano emits mostly hot ash and cinders.

Inside Story

If you could look deep inside a volcano, you would see magma, or hot melted rock, far below the surface. During a volcanic eruption extremely high pressure forces the magma up through vents, where it flows out—as lava. Gases, steam, ash, and other substances may also escape.

GASES, STEAM, ASH

LAVA FLOWS

CRATER

CENTRAL VENT

SIDE VENT

CRUST

MAGMA

TOM AND MICHELLE GRIMM / TONY STONE WORLDWIDE

About 600 active volcanoes dot the earth. They occur because earth's surface— "solid as a rock"—is actually in motion all the time. Earth's crust is made of plates, or huge, continent-size pieces. Where they collide or pull apart, magma rises and volcanoes occur. Sometimes they are destructive. They blast away mountains, bury cities and forests, and snuff out lives.

Volcanoes can also build islands and mountains. Their ash makes fertile soil, and their rock yields valuable minerals. In some places people use volcanic steam to heat homes. Scientists hope that radar images taken by the space shuttle *Endeavour* will provide clues about how volcanic eruptions affect earth's climate.

By Judith E. Rinard

ROGER RESSMEYER / STARLIGHT

Dust Busters

▲ *Yellow hard hats protect Japanese children from ash and debris erupting from Mount Sakurajima. This volcano has had many small eruptions since 1955. Students practice drills to evacuate in case of a major eruption.*

"Frozen" Solid

▲ *An old car, abandoned near a Hawaiian volcano, is trapped in stone. Flowing like hot taffy, lava gradually hardened around the car into layers of smooth black rock.*

Blast Off

▼ *A mile-wide crater tops Mount St. Helens in Washington State. Once a snowcapped peak, the volcano erupted so violently in 1980 it triggered huge landslides and blasted its top off.*

HOT STUFF

Volcanic Gems

Precious metals and diamonds come from ancient volcanic rock. Over millions of years gold and silver may form in veins, or narrow channels, as magma cools. Intense pressure inside volcanic rock squeezes carbon to form diamonds.

Old Geyser
Yellowstone National Park in Wyoming lies on top of a volcanic hot spot: Magma is relatively close to the earth's surface. Water heated underground builds up steam and gushes out through geysers, such as the world-famous Old Faithful.

KABOOM!
The Indonesian volcano Krakatau blew up in 1883. Its explosion was so loud people heard it 3,000 miles away.

Buried Alive
Mount Vesuvius in Italy erupted in A.D. 79. It covered the Roman city of Pompeii with 20 feet of ash. Centuries later archaeologists discovered houses, skeletons, and even food preserved under the ash.

Smoke Screen
The 1991 eruption of Mount Pinatubo in the Philippines sent a huge cloud of dust into the atmosphere. It made such a large haze that space shuttle astronauts orbiting the earth could not see the planet's surface clearly for several months after the eruption.

All Steamed Up

In Iceland people get steam for heating their homes and hot water for bathing from underground volcanic hot springs.

Ring of Fire
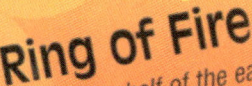
More than half of the earth's active volcanoes—about 300—lie in a chain that circles the Pacific Ocean. The chain is called the Ring of Fire.

WAYNE VINCENT

WEATHER
IS FULL of the NICEST
SOUNDS

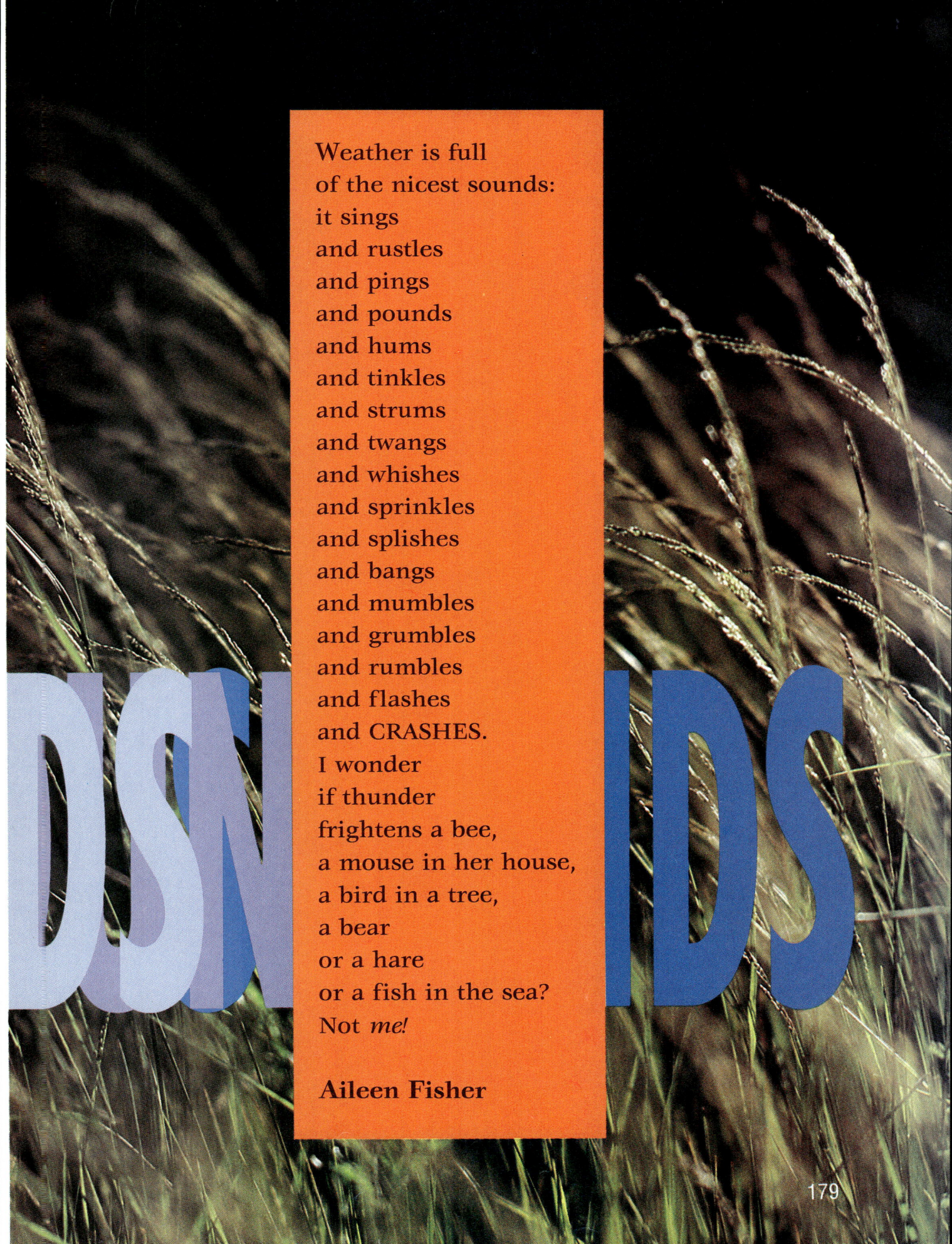

Weather is full
of the nicest sounds:
it sings
and rustles
and pings
and pounds
and hums
and tinkles
and strums
and twangs
and whishes
and sprinkles
and splishes
and bangs
and mumbles
and grumbles
and rumbles
and flashes
and CRASHES.
I wonder
if thunder
frightens a bee,
a mouse in her house,
a bird in a tree,
a bear
or a hare
or a fish in the sea?
Not *me!*

Aileen Fisher

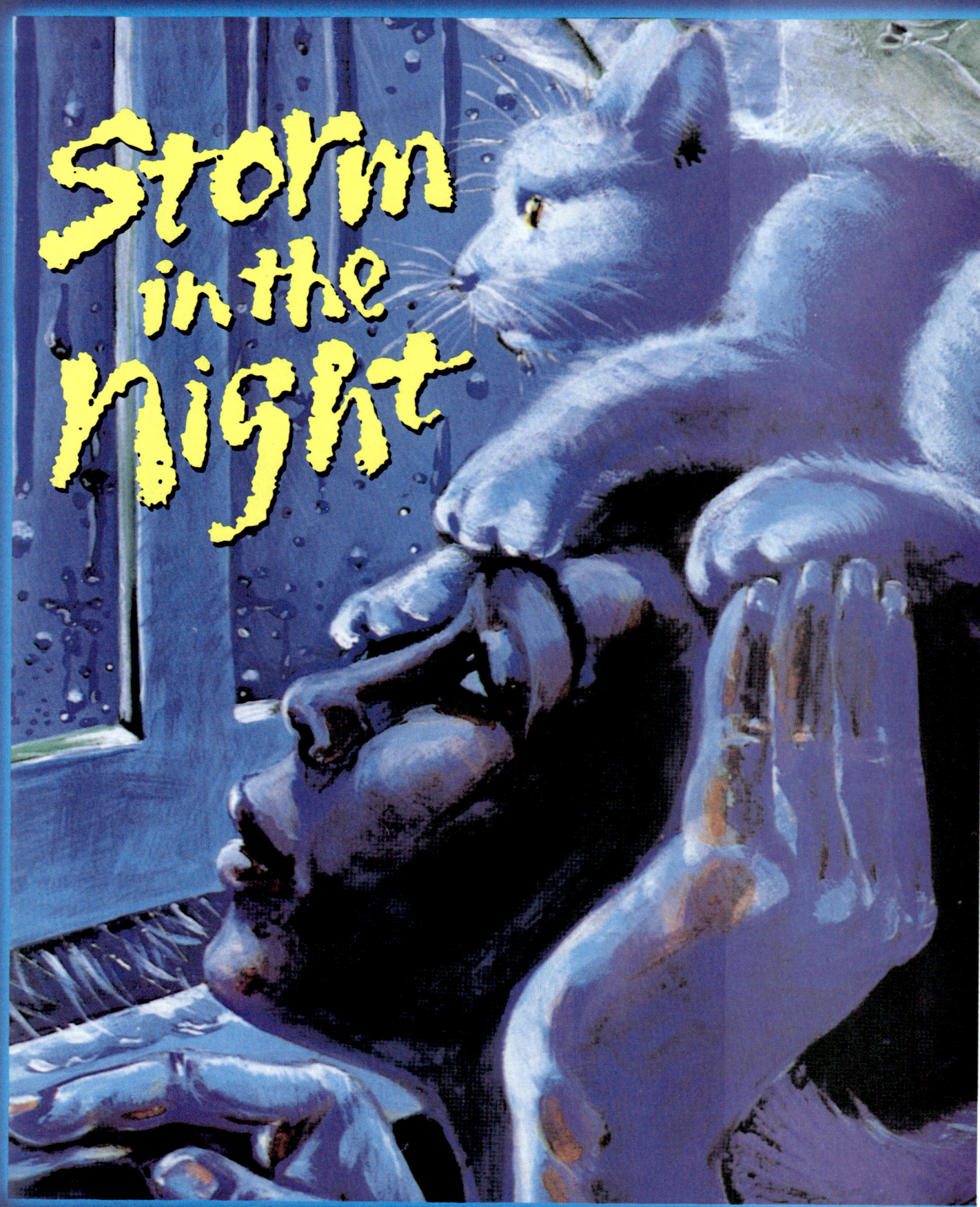

Storm in the Night

by Mary Stolz
illustrated by Pat Cummings

Storm in the night.

Thunder like mountains blowing up.

Lightning licking the navy-blue sky.

Rain streaming down the windows, babbling in the downspouts.

And Grandfather? . . . And Thomas? . . . And Ringo, the cat?

They were in the dark. Except for Ringo's shining mandarin eyes and the carrot-colored flames in the wood stove, they were quite in the dark.

"We can't read," said Grandfather.

"We can't look at TV," said Thomas.

"Too early to go to bed," said Grandfather.

Thomas sighed. "What will we do?"

"No help for it," said Grandfather, "I shall have to tell you a tale of when I was a boy."

Thomas smiled in the shadows. It was not easy to believe that Grandfather had once been a boy, but Thomas believed it. Because Grandfather said so, Thomas believed that long, long ago, probably at the beginning of the world, his grandfather had been a boy. As Thomas was a boy now, and always would be.

A grandfather could be a boy, if he went back in his memory far enough; but a boy could not be a grandfather.

Ringo could not grow up to be a kangaroo, and a boy could not grow up to be an old man.

And that, said Thomas to himself, is that.

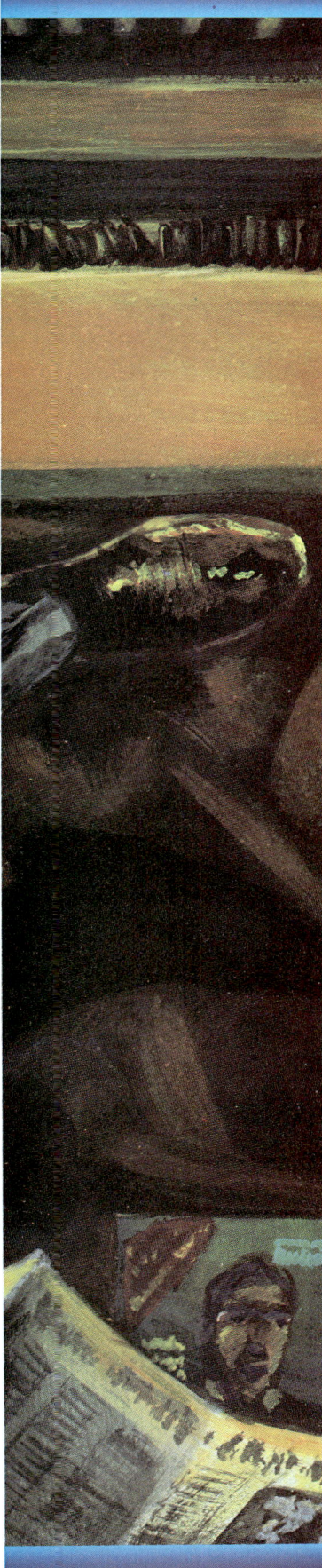

Grandfather was big and bearded.

Thomas had a chin as smooth as a peach.

Grandfather had a voice like a tuba.

Thomas's voice was like a penny whistle.

"I'm thinking," said Thomas.

"Ah," said Grandfather.

"I'm trying to think what you were like when you were my age."

"That's what I was like," said Grandfather.

"What?"

"Like someone your age."

"Did you look like me?"

"Very much like you."

"But you didn't have a beard."

"Not a sign of one."

"You were short, probably."

"Short, certainly."

"And your voice. It was like mine?"

"Exactly."

Thomas sighed. He just could not imagine it. He stopped trying. He tried instead to decide whether to ask for a new story or an old one.

Grandfather knew more stories than a book full of stories. Thomas hadn't heard all of them yet, because he kept asking for repeats.

As he thought about what to ask for, he listened to the sounds of the dark. Grandfather listened too.

In the house a door creaked. A faucet leaked.

Ringo scratched on his post, then on Grandfather's chair. He scratched behind his ear, and they could hear even that.

In the stove the flames made a fluttering noise.

"That's funny," said Thomas. "I can hear better in the dark than I can when the lights are on."

"No doubt because you are just listening," said his grandfather, "and not trying to see and hear at the same time."

That made sense to Thomas, and he went on listening for sounds in the dark.

There were the clocks.

The chiming clock on the mantel struck the hour of eight. *Ping, ping, ping, ping, ping, ping, ping, ping-a-ling.*

The kitchen clock, very excited. *Ticktickticktick-tick**tickety**.*

There were outside sounds for the listening, too.

The bells in the Congregational church rang through the rain. *Bong, bong, bong, bong, bong, bong, bong, BONG!*

Automobile tires swished on the rain-wet streets. Horns honked and hollered. A siren whined in the distance.

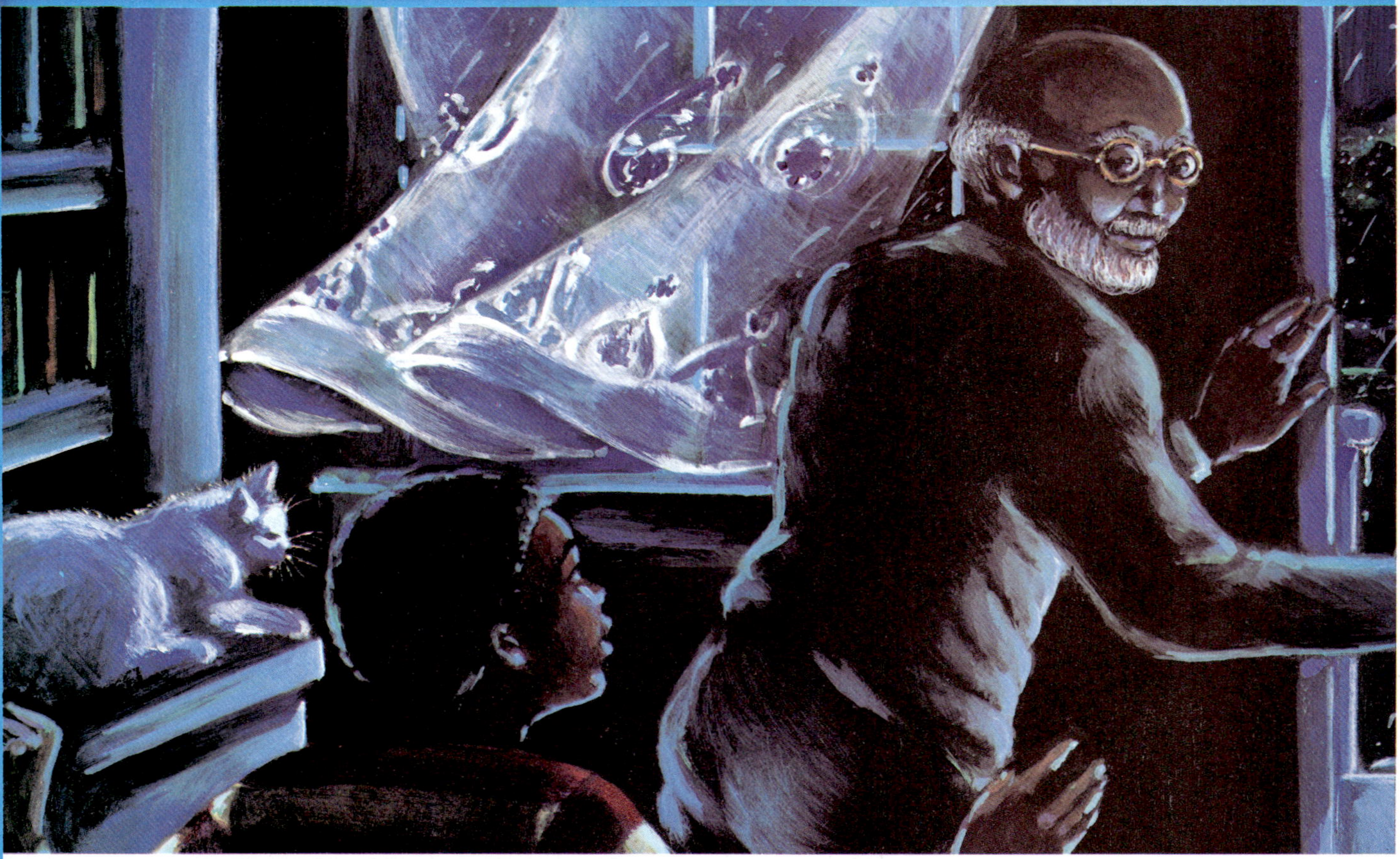

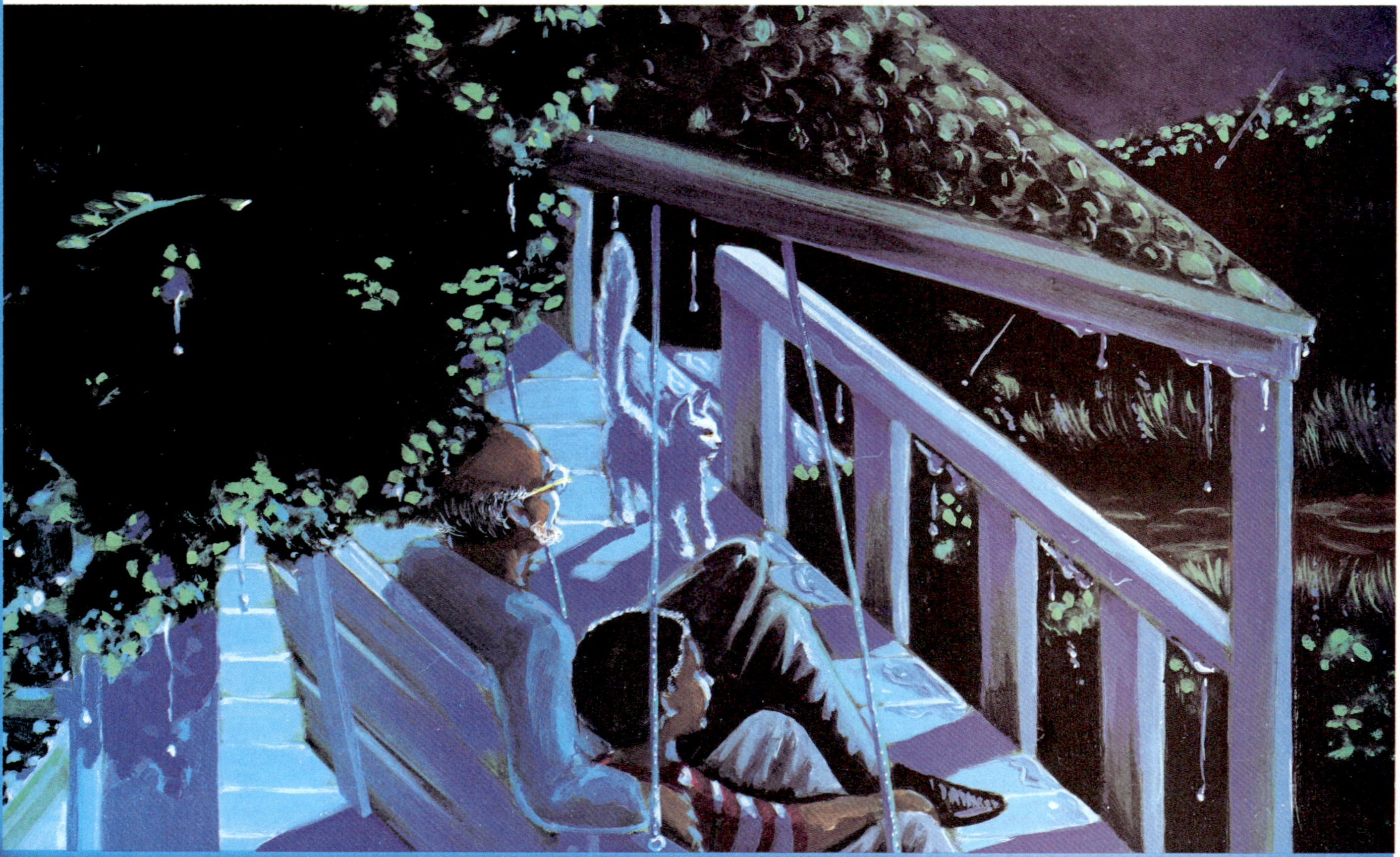

"Grandfather," said Thomas, "were there automobiles when you were a boy?"

"Were there *automobiles!*" Grandfather shouted. "How old do you think I am?"

"Well . . ." said Thomas.

"Next thing, you'll be asking if there was electricity when I was your age."

"Oh, Grandfather!" said Thomas, laughing. After a while he said, "Was there?"

"Let's go out on the porch," said Grandfather. "There's too much silliness in here."

By the light of the lightning they made their way to the front door and out on the porch. Ringo, who always followed Thomas, followed him and jumped to the railing.

The rain, driving hard against the back of the house, was scarcely sprinkling here. But it whooped windily through the great beech tree on the lawn, brandishing branches, tearing off twigs. It drenched the bushes, splashed in the birdbath, clattered on the tin roof like a million tacks.

Grandfather and Thomas sat on the swing, creaking back and forth, back and forth, as thunder boomed and lightning stabbed across the sky. Ringo's fur rose, and he turned his head from side to side, his eyes wide and wild in the flashes that lit up the night. The air smelled peppery and gardeny and new.

"That's funny," said Thomas. "I can smell better in the dark, too."

Thomas thought Grandfather answered, but he couldn't hear, as just then a bolt of lightning cracked into the big beech tree. It ripped off a mighty bough, which crashed to the ground. This was too much for Ringo. He leaped onto Thomas's lap and shivered there.

"Poor boy," said Thomas. "He's frightened."

"I had a dog when I was a boy," said Grandfather. "He was so scared of storms that I had to hide under the bed with him when one came. He was afraid even to be frightened alone."

"*I'm* not afraid of *anything,*" Thomas said, holding his cat close.

"Not many people can say that," said Grandfather. Then he added, "Well, I suppose anybody could *say* it."

"I'm not afraid of thunderstorms, like Ringo and your dog. What was his name?"

"Melvin."

"That's not a good name for a dog," Thomas said.

"I thought it was," Grandfather said calmly. "He was my dog."

"I like cats," said Thomas. "I want to own a *tiger!*"

"Not while you're living with me," said Grandfather.

"Okay," Thomas said. "Is there a story about Melvin?"

"There is. One very good one."

"Tell it," Thomas commanded. "Please, I mean."

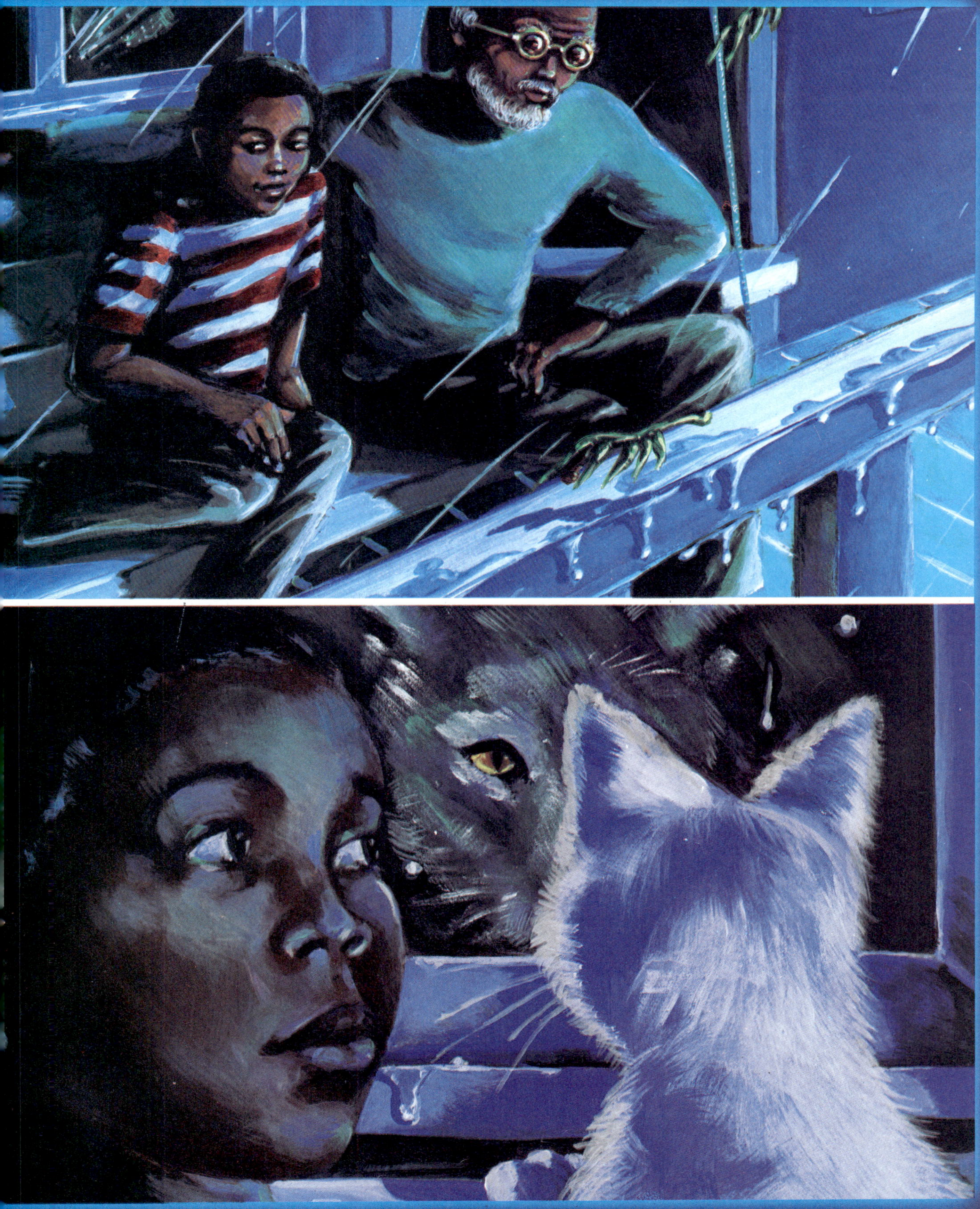

"Well," said Grandfather, "when Melvin and I were pups together, I was just as afraid of storms as he was."

"No!" said Thomas.

"Yes," said Grandfather. "We can't all be brave as tigers."

"I guess not," Thomas agreed.

"So there we were, the two of us, hiding under beds whenever a storm came."

"Think of that . . ." said Thomas.

"That's what I'm doing," said Grandfather. "Anyway, the day came when Melvin was out on some errand of his own, and I was doing my homework, when all at once, with only a rumble of warning . . . *down* came the rain, *down* came the lightning, and all around and everywhere came the thunder."

"Wow," said Thomas. "What did you do?"

"Dove under the bed."

"But what about Melvin?"

"I'm *coming* to that," said Grandfather. "What-about-Melvin is what the story is *about.*"

"I see," said Thomas. "This is pretty exciting."

"Well—it was then. Are you going to listen, or keep interrupting?"

"I think I'll listen," said Thomas.

"Good. Where was I?"

"Under the bed."

"So I was. Well, I lay there shivering at every clap of thunder, and

I'm ashamed to say that it was some time before I even remembered that my poor little dog was all by himself out in the storm."

Thomas shook his head in the dark.

"And when I did remember," Grandfather went on, "I had the most awful time making myself wriggle out from under the bed and go looking for my father or my mother—to ask them to go out and find Melvin for me."

"Grandfather!"

"I told you I was afraid. This is a true story you're hearing, so I have to tell the truth."

"Of course," said Thomas, admiring his grandfather for telling a truth like *that.* "Did you find them?"

"I did not. They had gone out someplace for an hour or so, but I'd forgotten. Thomas, fear does strange things to people . . . makes them forget everything but how afraid they are. You wouldn't know about that, of course."

Thomas stroked his cat and said nothing.

"In any case," Grandfather went on, "there I was, alone and afraid in the kitchen, and there was my poor little dog alone and afraid in the storm."

"What did you *do?*" Thomas demanded. "You didn't *leave* him out there, did you, Grandfather?"

"Thomas—I put on my raincoat and opened the kitchen door and stepped out on the back porch just as a flash of lightning

shook the whole sky and a clap of thunder barreled down and a huge man *appeared* out of the darkness, holding Melvin in his arms!"

"Whew!"

"That man was seven feet tall and had a face like a crack in the ice."

"Grandfather! You said you were telling me a true story."

"It's true, because that's how he looked to me. He stood there, scowling at me, and said, 'Son, is this your dog?' and I nodded, because I was too scared to speak. 'If you don't take better care of him, you shouldn't have him at all,' said the terrible man. He pushed Melvin at me and stormed off into the dark."

"Gee," said Thomas. "That wasn't very fair. He didn't know you were frightened too. I mean, Grandfather, how old were you?"

"Just about your age."

"Well, some people my age can get pretty frightened."

"Not you, of course."

Thomas said nothing.

"Later on," Grandfather continued, "I realized that man wasn't seven feet tall, or even terrible. He was worried about the puppy, so he didn't stop to think about me."

"Well, *I* think he should have."

"People don't always do what they should, Thomas."

"What's the end of the story?"

"Oh, just what you'd imagine," Grandfather said carelessly. "Having overcome my fear enough to forget myself and think about Melvin, I wasn't afraid of storms anymore."

"Oh, good," said Thomas.

For a while they were silent. The storm was spent. There were only flickers of lightning, mutterings of thunder, and a little patter of rain.

"When are the lights going to come on?" Thomas asked.

"You know as much as I do," said Grandfather.

"Maybe they won't come on for hours," said Thomas. "Maybe they won't come on until *tomorrow!*"

"Maybe not."

"Maybe they'll *never* come on again, and what will we do then?"

"We'll think of something," said Grandfather.

"Grandfather?"

"Yes, Thomas?"

"What I think . . . I think that maybe if you hadn't been here, and Ringo hadn't been here, and I was all alone in the house and there was a storm and the lights went out and didn't come on again for a long time, like this . . . I think maybe *then* I would be a *little* bit afraid."

"Perfectly natural," said Grandfather.

Thomas sighed.

Grandfather yawned.

Ringo jumped to the porch floor and walked daintily into the garden, shaking his legs.

After a while the lights came on.

They turned them off and went to bed.

meet Mary Stolz

For Mary Stolz, *Storm in the Night* was a dream come true. "What I wished for was a book that would show at once a peaceful, cozy companionship—the boy, the grandfather, the cat—and an understanding of fear," she explains.

People often ask Stolz the secret to becoming a writer. She replies, "My one-word recipe is READ."

and Pat Cummings

Pat Cummings likes thunderstorms, so she enjoyed painting the pictures for *Storm in the Night*. It took her a year to complete the work.

Cummings has been drawing all her life. When she was a child, she loved to draw ballerinas. Today, she invites children she meets to send her their drawings. She tells them, "Keep drawing. Don't let anyone talk you out of it."

IN TIME OF

Silver Rain

In time of silver rain
The earth
Puts forth new life again,
Green grasses grow
And flowers lift their heads,
And over all the plain
The wonder spreads
    Of life,
    Of life,
    Of life!

In time of silver rain
The butterflies
Lift silken wings
To catch a rainbow cry,
And trees put forth
New leaves to sing
In joy beneath the sky
As down the roadway
Passing boys and girls
Go singing, too,
In time of silver rain
    When spring
    And life
    Are new.

Langston Hughes

Unit 3

TEAMWORK

Dream Wolf

by Paul Goble

In the old days the people travelled over the plains. They followed the great herds of buffalo.

Every year when the berries were ripe, they would leave the plains and go up into the hills. They made camp in a valley where the berry bushes grow. Everyone picked great quantities. They mashed the berries into little cakes which they dried in the sun. These they stored in painted bags for the winter.

Tiblo (tee-blow) was too young to play with the older boys. He and his little sister, Tanksi (tawnk-she), had to go berry-picking with their mother and the other women and children.

207

Tiblo was soon tired of picking, and too full to eat any more. When nobody was looking he slipped away with Tanksi to climb the hills.

They climbed up and up among the rocks and cedar trees where bighorn sheep and bears live. Soon they could hardly hear the berry-pickers laughing and calling to each other far below. Tiblo wanted to reach the top. They climbed on.

They never noticed the sun starting to go down behind the hills.

It was getting dark when Tiblo knew they had to go back home. In the twilight every hill and valley looked the same. He did not know which way to go. He called out. . . . Only the echoes answered him.

They wandered on. Tiblo was lost. Darkness closed around them. It grew colder. They were tired and hungry, and Tanksi began to cry.

Speaking of happy things, Tiblo found a small cave among the rocks. They crawled inside to shelter for the night.

The children were tired, and in a little while they fell asleep. Tiblo had a dream.

He dreamed that a wolf with shining eyes entered the cave. In his dream he felt the wolf's hot breath and its rough tongue licking his face. The wolf lay down beside him. His shaggy fur was like a blanket which kept Tiblo and Tanksi warm.

The sun was already shining into the mouth of the cave when Tiblo opened his eyes again.

Tiblo woke up his sister. They crawled out of the cave into the warm sunshine. He took Tanksi by the hand, and they set off walking down the hill.

When the children came to a stream, they stopped to drink. Suddenly Tiblo saw that a wolf was sitting on some rocks close by, watching them. At once he remembered his dream.

"O Wolf," Tiblo said, "we are lost. Mother will be crying. Help us to find our way home again."

The wolf panted and smiled. "My children, do not worry. I will help you. Last night you slept in my den. Follow me now, and I will take you home."

214

The wolf trotted off. He looked back to see that the children were following. From time to time he trotted ahead out of sight, but he always returned.

At last the wolf led them to a hilltop. The children were filled with joy to see their home in the valley below. The wolf sat back on his haunches and smiled. And then he trotted off back toward the hills. The children begged him to come and live with them.

"No," the wolf called back, "I like to wander from place to place with my friends. Listen for me in the evenings! You will hear me calling, and you will know that I never forget you."

People in the camp saw the children coming down the hill. The men jumped on to their horses, and galloped out to bring them home. Everyone was happy that the children were safe.

217

Tiblo told how the wolf had brought them home. Everyone walked into the hills to thank the wolf. They spread a blanket for him to sit on. They gave him necklaces and other beautiful gifts.

There has been close kinship with the Wolf People for as long as anyone can remember. That is what they say.

The wolves are no longer heard calling
in the evenings at berry-picking time. Hunters
have killed and driven them away with guns
and traps and poisons. People say that the
wolves will return when we, like Tiblo and
Tanksi, have the wolves in our hearts and
dreams again.

Meet Paul Goble

When Paul Goble was growing up in England, he was interested in Native Americans. To him, their world seemed very different from the "crowded island" where he lived. Later, Goble visited the United States. He stayed with Sioux friends in South Dakota and Crow friends in Montana. When they saw how much he loved their ways, they taught him about their beliefs and folklore. Goble turned what he learned into books. One, *The Girl Who Loved Wild Horses,* received a Caldecott Medal in 1979.

In his books, Paul Goble tries to show what wild animals are really like. He is upset by mistaken ideas about them, such as the notion that "bears are huggable, woodpeckers are destructive, coyotes and tomcats mean." He admires the Native Americans' belief that animals deserve respect because they were on the earth before people.

Paul Goble explains that he has learned many wonderful things from Native American people. He says, "I have simply wanted to express and to share these things which I love so much."

THE GIRL WHO LOVED WILD HORSES
by PAUL GOBLE

The Wolves of Winter

Many people have the wrong picture of wolves. Photographer Jim Brandenburg wants to change the animals' image.

Gray wolves hide from people. Jim Brandenburg has spent 25 years photographing them in their natural habitat. He has learned to avoid eye contact because wolves are easily scared away.

BOYS' LIFE

THE AGE OF ARMOR

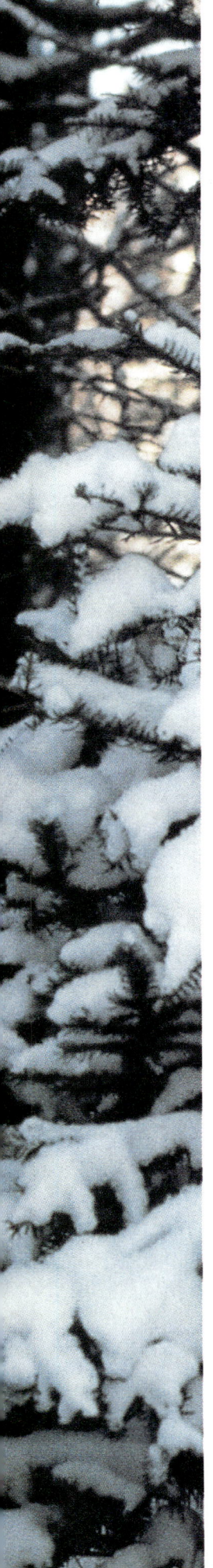

*S*nowshoeing across a frozen lake in Minnesota, photographer Jim Brandenburg couldn't believe his eyes. Trotting straight toward him was a gray wolf.

Brandenburg dropped to the ice, aimed his camera—and waited. Did the wolf see him? Yes. It advanced slowly toward the funny-looking lump on the ground.

"Maybe it's a dead moose for dinner," the wolf may have been thinking.

Suddenly, the wolf stopped, realizing that Jim was human. The animal seemed embarrassed.

"The wolf simply walked away," Jim said. "He looked at me over his shoulder once like, 'Oh, *no!* I can't *believe* it!'"

Brandenburg was sorry to see the wolf go, but not surprised. After 25 years of photographing wolves, he knows they are shy around people.

Big, Bad Wolf

As a boy, Jim held the common view that wolves are bad. But by reading and observing, he learned that they are a valuable part of the wilderness. They cull weak and sick animals and help preserve the balance of nature.

Wolves may fiercely hunt deer, elk and other prey, but they would rather run away than face a human. (Like all wild animals, they should be treated with respect and caution.)

To keep from scaring the wolves, Jim moves slowly when photographing them. He watches their actions to see if they've been startled. He avoids eye contact and pretends to ignore them.

"You kind of have to pretend you're a cow munching on some grass," he says.

Wolves Are Smart

Wolves belong to packs, as we belong to families. A pack usually has a mother, father and three to six offspring that hunt and play together.

223

Each pack considers a certain area its territory—and will protect it against other wolves.

Wolves "talk" to each other. They whimper to express friendliness. They howl to call the pack together or to warn away another wolf or pack. Their howls can be heard from 10 miles away.

A younger wolf submits to the pack's leader, or "alpha male."

Wolves are clever hiders.

"Many times I'll be in the woods," Brandenburg says, "and I'll know that a wolf is there—I'll either hear it or see its tracks—but I'll never see it." So Jim has had to be clever too.

He started by building a cabin in wolf country, the boundary waters area near Ely, Minn. It is the only region in the lower 48 states (outside Alaska) where large numbers of wolves live. But just being there wasn't enough.

Sometimes Jim would drag a deer killed by a car into his yard. That might draw hungry wolves in close enough to photograph. Other times Jim would track a pack for days, following the wolves' paw prints, as they stalked their prey. He would even howl at the wolves and listen to their reply to see how close they were. The more time he spent stalking wolves, the better he got at it.

Winter Hunters

While many animals, including squirrels and some bears, hibernate in winter, wolves don't. They stay awake, hunting. Their soft, snowshoe-like paws keep them from sinking in frozen snow. The graceful predator can attack big game like elk or moose clumsily trying to flee. Wolves might even attack a hibernating bear. Most wouldn't dare do that when the bear is awake.

Patience and Good Luck

Jim must be patient to get photos. Sometimes he goes for weeks without shooting a picture. Other times he gets lucky. Once, a mother wolf let him peek inside her den, where pups were sleeping.

Brandenburg wants his photographs to tell the real story of wolves. Then, people might not fear them so. And perhaps someday more of our country will be like Minnesota, where wild wolves roam free.

—*Rachel Buchholz*

Wolves Are Coming Back

North America is home to the gray (or "timber") wolf and the red wolf (which may be a wolf/coyote mix).

After almost being wiped out by man, wolves are recovering. About 57,000 gray wolves now live in Canada and Alaska; another 2,000 survive in the lower 48 states. Most of those live in Minnesota. Red wolves may number fewer than 100. Almost all have been moved to North Carolina.

Some people want to speed their recovery by moving wolves back into areas they used to roam, including Yellowstone National Park in Wyoming. Some ranchers and hunters oppose the effort, saying wolves would kill livestock, deer and elk.

Wolves travel, hunt, play and defend their territory as a family, or pack.

Wolves play games with each other. This pair appears to be playing "tag."

A pack feeds on a deer it killed.

225

OPERATION RESC

from 3-2-1 Contact

SAVING SEA LIFE FROM OIL SPILLS

Sea otters look for danger by standing tall in the water, shading their eyes with their forefeet. But their natural watchfulness couldn't help the otters of Prince William Sound in Alaska one day in 1989.

That's when the oil tanker *Exxon Valdez* hit an underwater reef, causing the worst oil spill ever in U.S. waters. About 11 million gallons gushed into the Alaskan sound, spoiling 304 miles of shoreline.

Whether it's a big spill like the one in Alaska, or smaller ones that have taken place in other parts of the U.S.—a spill can be deadly for the animals who get caught in it. Whales, seals and sea lions seem to get through a spill without much damage because they have blubber to keep warm.

But others, such as sea otters and seabirds, suffer badly. They need help quickly

UE

by Christina Wilsdon

—or they will freeze to death in the cold ocean water.

"Otters need their thick fur to keep them warm," explains Jim Robinett. He is a marine mammal expert at the Shedd Aquarium in Chicago, Illinois. If an otter's fur gets dirty—or coated with oil—that means danger. The hairs can't help hold warm air next to the body —or keep freezing water out.

"Some birds are so badly coated with oil that it's hard to tell what kinds they are," says Marge Gibson, who runs the Orange County Bird of Prey Rescue Center in Villa Park, California. "You just see this blob with its eyes blinking, and you realize it's alive."

That's when professional animal handlers—and volunteers—get to work. Thanks to these dedicated people, thousands of animals have been saved.

Saving otters starts with scooping them out of the water with long-handled nets. After they are caught, rescuers start to clean the animals. This isn't the easiest job. Big otters can weigh 80 pounds. Their jaws can crush bones. And they move very fast. "We call them 'Slinkies covered with fur,'" says Robinett. "They seem to turn around inside their skins!"

A light dose of anesthesia slows an otter down so that it can be handled, yet be awake. Still, it takes four people to wash one otter.

"Washing" means scrubbing the otter with water and dish soap for 30 to 40 minutes. The otter lies on a screen over a tub made out of half an oil drum. The oily, soapy water drains into the drum. Then the animal is rinsed for 20 to 30 minutes until the soap is gone.

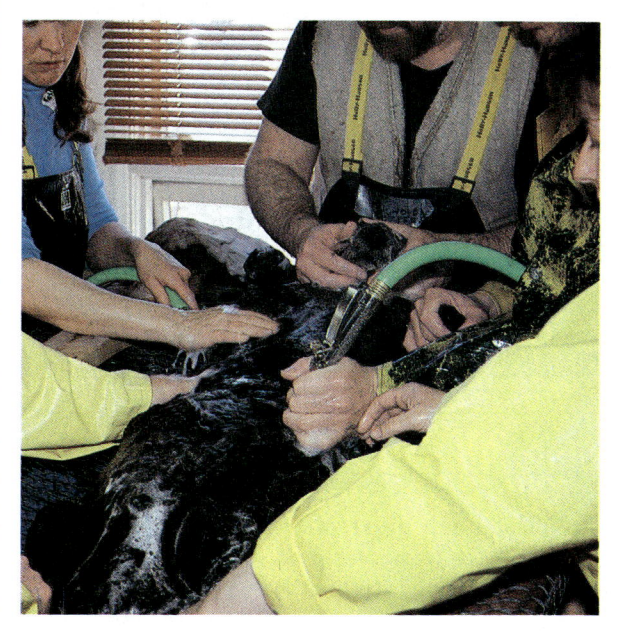

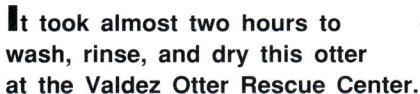

It took almost two hours to wash, rinse, and dry this otter at the Valdez Otter Rescue Center.

Oiled otters also have their insides cleaned out. That's because they often swallow oil as they try to lick themselves clean. Oil damages an animal's liver and kidneys. "We tube-feed them a solution that absorbs the poisonous oil that may be in the intestines," explains Robinett. "The solution has tiny bits of charcoal, similar to what people use in a home aquarium."

Next, the otter goes to "intensive care"—an indoor pen filled with soft towels. Even though it survived the oil—as well as the "wash-and-rinse cycle"—the otter is still at risk. When the otter is out of danger, rescuers move it outdoors to a dry pen.

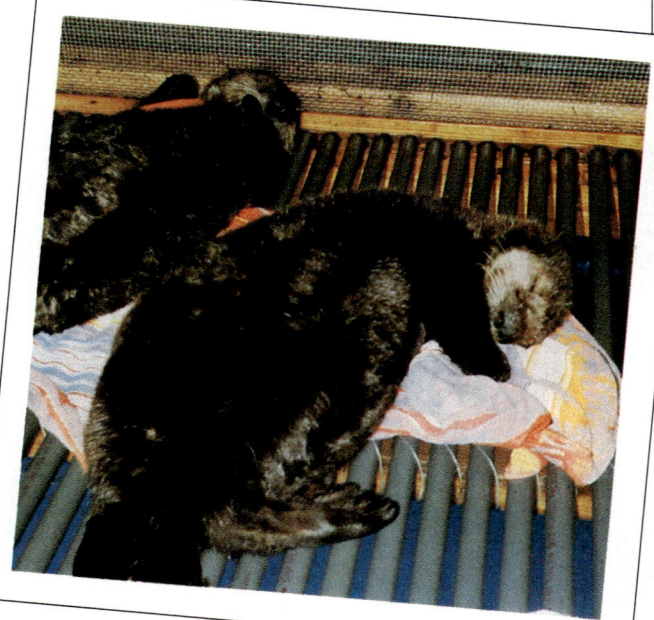

The oil spill left these otter pups orphans. After being rescued, one pup sleeps with a security blanket. *(Left)*

A cleaned pup is held by a volunteer before being released. *(Above)*

It's playtime! Recovering pups have fun in the swimming pool. *(Opposite page)*

Otters also get daily trips to a swimming pool. This way, the otter can groom and clean itself. "Grooming helps produce natural oils, which coat the fur and help create the insulating layer that otters depend on," says Robinett.

Veterinarians, zoo and aquarium keepers keep track of the otter's temperature and food intake. Finally, when it's healthy, the otter is moved into a sea pen where it stays until it's strong enough to be released.

BIRDS OF A FEATHER

Seabirds suffer many of the same problems that otters do, but they need different care because they are more delicate.

"A rescued bird is weak," says Nicolette Heaphy, who works at the International Bird Rescue Research Center in Berkeley, California. "It needs fluids, which are tube-fed into its stomach. We place the birds in a pen and don't wash them for 24 hours. They've been through a lot of stress. Washing them in that situation can kill them."

The birds don't get anesthesia or charcoal solution. But they do get a cloth bib to wear around their necks. The bib keeps them from trying to clean, or preen, their feathers. "They preen and preen," says Heaphy. "They just don't understand that the oil isn't removeable."

Seabirds preen because they depend on their feathers to keep them warm and dry. Each feather has many barbs that hook into each other. Plus, the feathers overlap like shingles on a roof. "Many people think a bird is naturally waterproofed," says Heaphy. "Not so. It's the interlocking barbs that create a kind of wetsuit."

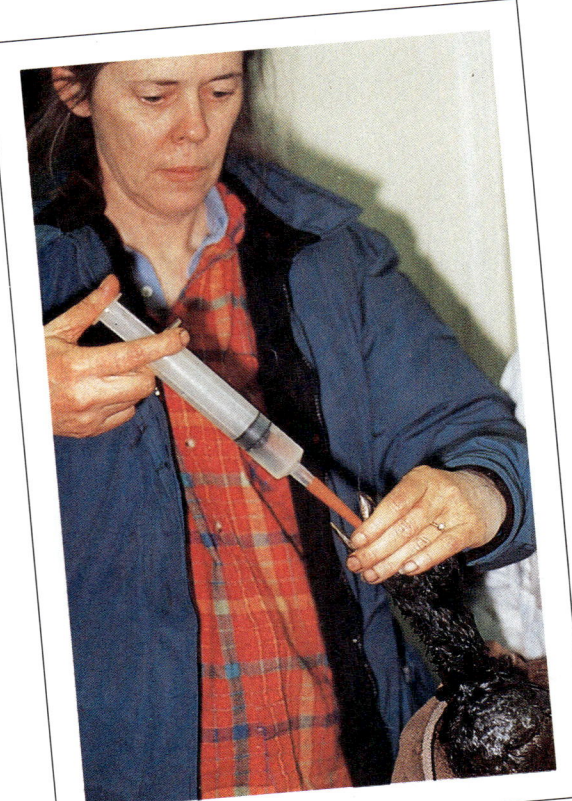

Volunteers feed a mixture of liquid fish food and vitamins by tube into the mouth of an oiled bird. *(Left)*

If workers miss a spot, the bird could freeze to death in the cold Alaskan waters. *(Right)*

Oil stuck in the barbs prevents the feathers from locking together. Cold water seeps in, soaking the downy feathers that normally hold warm air. It reaches the skin—and soon the bird freezes to death.

Scrubbing a bird would break its feathers. So a team of two washers must use a different method. They place the bird in tub after tub of soapy dish water, pouring cupfuls of water over its body and wings. Then workers use a

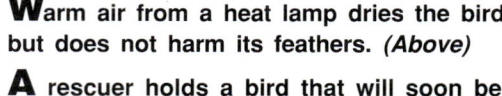

Warm air from a heat lamp dries the bird but does not harm its feathers. *(Above)*

A rescuer holds a bird that will soon be set free. *(Right)*

soft toothbrush and an electric tooth cleaner to remove oil from the bird's head.

Next, rescuers rinse the bird by forcing jets of water through its feathers. "Detergent is as bad for keeping the feathers waterproofed as oil is," explains Heaphy. So it's important to get all the soap out.

Strangely enough, the bird looks drier the more it is rinsed. This is because its outer feathers start to lock together again. But the downy feathers underneath are still wet. So the bird is put in a pen and dried with warm air.

"Then the bird is put in a pool to check its waterproofing," explains Heaphy. "Leftover soap or oil will show up as wet spots on the body." Birds that are not waterproofed go back for re-rinsing.

Birds that pass the waterproofing tests are not released right away. They must also be eating well. Their weight and blood are checked, too. When all the medical signs are right, they are banded and set free.

AGAINST ALL ODDS

OPERATION RESCUE 14

The *Valdez* spill left a sad story behind. More than 1,000 otters and more than 30,000 dead seabirds were found. Many others died and were never found. Scientists think that as many as 250,000 birds were killed.

But the rescue workers all speak of the joy they felt when their hard work ended in the release of healthy animals. "The success stories meant a lot to us because so many birds and otters died," biologist James Styers told *3-2-1 Contact*. "Saving any individual animal was worth all the work."

MEET CHRISTINA WILSDON

Christina Wilsdon writes for several children's magazines, including *Electric Company* and *3-2-1 Contact*. About a year after the big 1989 oil spill in Alaska, Wilsdon began to work on an article about that spill. Her desire to write the article came from her lifelong love of animals and her interest in the environment. She hoped to show readers how scientists and volunteers worked together to save the wildlife. She also wanted to help people understand "how precious and beautiful this world is."

235

GOING,

There is bad news and good news in the animal world. The bad news is that many animals are in danger of becoming extinct. The good news is that people are doing things to save some of these animals.

The Bald Eagle

THE BAD NEWS When it was named our national bird in 1782, the bald eagle ranged over all of North America. But until recently it had almost disappeared. Chemicals had polluted the waters in which eagles hunted for fish. People had destroyed many nesting places.

THE GOOD NEWS Some of the polluting chemicals were banned. People began to protect some of the eagles' nesting places and to raise eagles and then set them free. Now, more and more bald eagles are being spotted across the nation.

Red Wolf
Five hundred years ago, thousands of red wolves roamed the southeastern United States. By the early 1990s, only 133 red wolves were left.

African Elephant
In the early 1980s, scientists counted about 1,500,000 African elephants in zoos and on the African plains. Today, only 400,000 survive.

GOING...

The Panda Bear

THE BAD NEWS In 1980, only a thousand giant pandas were left in the wild. Much of the bamboo on which they depend for food had died or been cut down. People were also killing pandas for their fur. The giant pandas were running out of time.

THE GOOD NEWS The remaining bamboo forests are now protected, and new ones are being planted. Laws have been passed to keep people from hunting pandas. The giant panda is still endangered, but now there is hope for the future.

Golden Lion Tamarin
In 1974, only 174 golden lion tamarins were still alive. Now there are about 500 in zoos and about 200 in Brazilian forests.

American Bison
In 1850, twenty million bison thundered across the North American plains. By 1889, only 551 were left in the United States. Today, about 30,000 bison live in parks.

The Toad

I found me a hoptoad
Sitting in the yard.
I tried to watch him,
But watching him was hard.
He hopped in the road
With one big hop,
And I called out, "Toad,
Stop!
Stop!"

"Toad," I yelled,
"Get out of the road.
Here comes a truck
With a mighty heavy load!"

The truck came a-racketing
And roaring on,
And just as I thought:
"There's a good toad gone,"
S l o w l y
The toad hopped onto the lawn.

The toad acted sleepy
As the truck went by,
And while he rested
And blinked a beady eye,
My ears heard a whirring,
And my nose smelled gas,
And up came Willie,
Gaily mowing grass.

The wheels of the power-mower
Never once slowed;
And—suddenly scared—
I shouted, "Toad,
Hurry up.
Hop!
Or you'll get mowed!"

"A mower," I told him,
Trying hard to talk,
"Can grind up a toad
Like a dandelion stalk."
The toad peered over
A bud of white clover
And s l o w l y
Hopped on the flagstone walk.

That was the second thing
But still not the last.
After a minute
A puppy lolloped past.
I drove off the puppy,
And I scatted a cat,
And I took the toad
To the woods
After that.

I like being helpful,
And I'm no quitter,
But *that* toad needed
A baby sitter.

Kaye Starbird

Meet
Yoshiko Uchida

Yoshiko Uchida grew up with two cultures. One was the culture that surrounded her home in California. The other consisted of the Japanese customs and traditions of her parents.

Uchida says, "I feel it's so important for Japanese-American—and all Asian-American—children to be aware of their history and culture. . . . At the same time, I write for *all* children, and I try to write about values and feelings that are universal."

Yoshiko Uchida wrote her very first book, *Jimmy Chipmonk and His Friends: A Short Story for Small Children,* at age ten. Animals appear in some of the writings she's done as an adult, too, such as *The Two Foolish Cats* and *The Rooster Who Understood Japanese.*

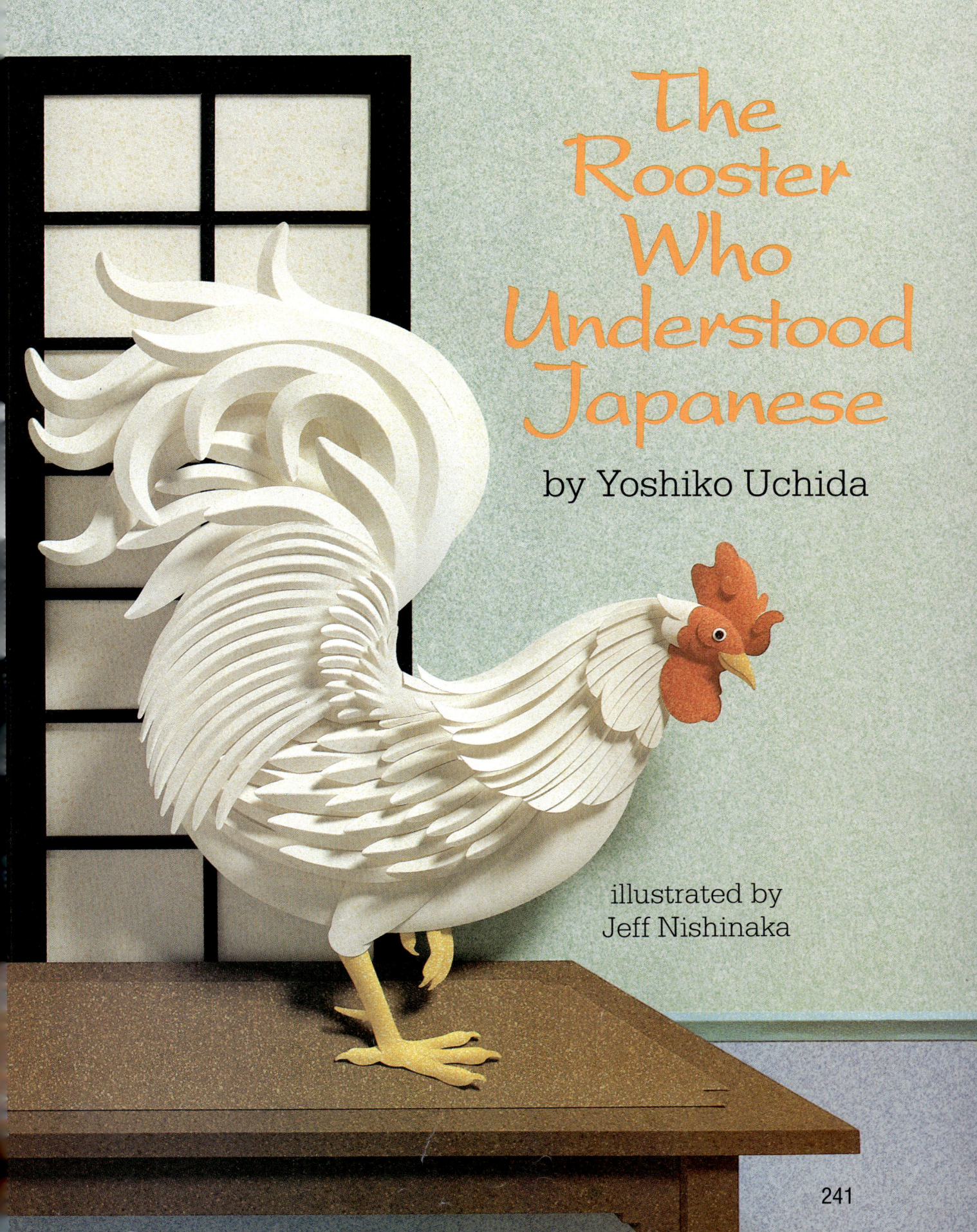

The Rooster Who Understood Japanese

by Yoshiko Uchida

illustrated by Jeff Nishinaka

"Mrs. K.!" Miyo called. "I'm here!"

Every afternoon when Miyo came home from school, where she was in the third grade, she went to the home of her neighbor, Mrs. Kitamura, whom she called "Mrs. K."

This was because Miyo's mother was a doctor at University Hospital and didn't get home until supper time. Sometimes, she didn't get home even then, and if she didn't, Miyo just stayed on at Mrs. K's.

It was a fine arrangement all around because Mrs. Kitamura was a widow, and she enjoyed Miyo's company. Not that she was lonely. She had a basset hound named Jefferson, a ten-year-old parrot named Hamilton, a coal black cat named Leonardo, and a pet rooster named Mr. Lincoln. She talked to all of them in Japanese. She also talked to the onions and potatoes she'd planted in her front yard instead of a lawn, coaxing them each day to grow plump and delicious.

Miyo stopped next to see Mr. Lincoln. He was strutting about in his pen making rooster-like sounds and looking very intelligent and dignified. Mrs. K. had told Miyo that he understood every word she said to him whether she spoke in English or Japanese.

"Mrs. Kitamura, *doko?*" Miyo said, asking Mr. Lincoln where she was.

He cocked his head, looked at her with his small bright eyes, and uttered a squawking sound.

Miyo shrugged. Maybe Mr. Lincoln did understand Japanese, but it certainly didn't do her any good if she couldn't understand what he said back to her.

"Never mind," she said. "I'll find her." And she hurried toward the brown shingled

house covered with ivy that hung over it like droopy hair. The back door was unlatched, and Miyo walked in.

"Mrs. K., I'm here," she called once more.

Immediately a high shrill voice repeated, "Mrs. K., I'm here." It was Hamilton, the parrot, who lived in a big gold cage in Mrs. Kitamura's kitchen.

"Hello, Hamilton," Miyo said.

"Hello, Hamilton," he answered back.

Miyo sniffed as she walked through the kitchen, hoping she might smell chocolate brownies or freshly baked bread. But today there were no nice welcoming smells at all. There was only silence and the smell of floor wax.

Miyo went through the swinging doors into the dining room and found Mrs. K. sitting at the big oval dining room table. She still wore her floppy gardening hat over the pile of gray hair that had been frizzled by a home permanent, and she was doing something Miyo had never seen her do before. She was making herself a cup of ceremonial Japanese tea, whipping up the special powdered green tea in a beautiful tea bowl with a small bamboo whisk.

Miyo knew exactly what Mrs. K. was doing because she had seen a lady in a silk kimono perform the

Japanese tea ceremony at the Buddhist temple just last month.

Somehow Mrs. K. didn't look quite right preparing the tea in her gardening smock and floppy hat, sitting at a table piled high with old newspapers and magazines. Furthermore, she was frowning, and Miyo knew the tea ceremony was supposed to make one feel peaceful and calm.

"*Mah!*" Mrs. K. said, looking startled. "I was so busy with my thoughts, I didn't even hear you come in."

Miyo looked at the pale green froth of tea in the tea bowl, knowing it was strong and bitter. "Is that our afternoon tea?" she asked, trying not to look too disappointed.

"No, no, not yours," Mrs. K. answered
quickly. "Just mine. I made it to calm
myself." She turned the bowl around
carefully and drank it in the proper three
and a half sips. "There," she sighed.

"Are you calm now?"

Mrs. K. shook her head. "Not really.
Actually, not at all. As a matter of fact, I am
most upset."

Mrs. Kitamura stood up and started toward the kitchen, and Leonardo appeared from beneath her chair to follow close behind. Miyo thought that was a strange name for a cat, but Mrs. K. had told her he was a very sensitive, creative cat, and she had named him after Leonardo da Vinci.

In fact, all of Mrs. K's pets had very elegant and dignified names which she had chosen after going to a class in American history in order to become an American citizen. She said animals were purer in spirit than most human beings and deserved names that befit their character. "Besides," she had added, "I like to be different."

Mrs. K. certainly was different, all right. She wasn't at all like most of the other elderly ladies who went to the Japanese Buddhist temple.

"It is because I am a free spirit," she had explained to Miyo one day.

Maybe it was because she had lived in America so much longer than the other ladies who had come from Japan. She never did anything she didn't want to do, although she was always careful not to cause anyone any grief.

Miyo wondered now why Mrs. K. was so upset.

Usually she was full of fun, but today she scarcely smiled at Miyo.

"I've been upset since seven o'clock this morning," she explained suddenly.

"Why?" Miyo asked, gratefully accepting a glass of milk and some peanut butter cookies. "Did you get out of the wrong side of bed?"

That was what her mother sometimes asked when Miyo was grumpy. But that wasn't Mrs. K's trouble at all.

"It's not me," she said. "It's my new neighbor, Mr. Wickett. He told me that if Mr. Lincoln didn't stop waking him up by crowing at six in the morning, he was going to report me to the police for disturbing the peace! Can you imagine anything so unfriendly?"

Miyo certainly couldn't. "He's mean," she said.

"What am I going to do?" Mrs. K. asked, as though Miyo were the wise old woman in the Japanese tale who could answer any puzzling question put to her.

"I can't go out and tell Mr. Lincoln he is not to crow anymore. That would be like telling Jefferson not to wag his tail, or telling Leonardo not to groom himself . . ."

"Or telling Hamilton not to mimic us," Miyo said, getting into the spirit of things.

"Exactly," Mrs. K. agreed. "He is only behaving in his natural rooster-like way. And besides," she added, "any respectable old man should be up by six o'clock. You and your mama have never complained."

Miyo didn't say that they were already up at six o'clock anyway. She wondered what she could say to make Mrs. K. feel better, and finally she said, "I'll ask my mother. She'll know what to do."

Miyo's mother usually found a way to solve most problems. She had to because Miyo had no father, and there was no one else in their house to ask. Miyo's father had died long ago and Miyo barely remembered him.

"Don't worry, Mama will think of something," Miyo said as she left Mrs. Kitamura's house.

Mrs. K. nodded. "I hope so," she said dismally. "In the meantime, I must think of something before six o'clock tomorrow morning."

When Miyo got home, Mother was just
starting supper. "Hi sweetie," she called.
"How was Mrs. K.?"

"She was worried," Miyo answered as
she began to set the table. "She's got to
make Mr. Lincoln stop crowing."

"Whatever for?"

Miyo quickly told Mother about Mr. Wickett. "He's a mean old man," she said, scowling at the thought of him. "Mr. Lincoln doesn't hurt anybody."

But Mother said, "Well, I can see Mr. Wickett's side too. If I could sleep late, I'm not so sure I'd like having a rooster wake me at six o'clock. Besides," she added, "our town is growing, and we're in the city limits now. Maybe Mrs. K. will just have to give Mr. Lincoln away."

Miyo didn't even want to think of such a thing. "But he's not just any old rooster," she objected.

He certainly wasn't. Mrs. K. had raised him since he was a baby chick, thinking that he was going to become a hen and give her an egg for breakfast every day.

"Besides," she added, "he doesn't crow very loud."

Mother nodded sympathetically. "I know," she said. "Well, maybe we can think of something."

But nobody could. Not mother, not Miyo, nor Mrs. K.

That first night Mrs. K. brought Mr. Lincoln inside the house and stuffed him into a big cardboard carton in her bedroom.

"Poor Mr. Lincoln," she said to Miyo the next day. "He nearly smothered, and I hardly got any sleep at all. He crowed in the morning anyway, but I don't think

Mr. Wickett heard him because so far the police haven't come. But I jump every time my doorbell rings. What on earth are we going to do?" she asked, wrapping Miyo into the bundle of her troubles.

Miyo wished she had an answer, but all she could say was, "Mama and I are both thinking hard."

Mrs. K. had been so worried she had spent the entire day cooking Japanese food to take her mind off her troubles.

"I made two kinds of *osushi* today," she said to Miyo, showing her an enormous platter of flavored rice rolled in sheets of seaweed. She had also cooked slices of fried bean curd and stuffed them with rice so they looked like fox ears. Mrs. K. had been pouring her worries into the fox ears all morning, but like her potatoes and onions, they couldn't tell her what to do.

Mrs. K. gave Miyo a platter of *osushi* when she left. "Take some home for your supper," she said. "Your mama will be glad not to have to cook tonight."

Miyo felt that neither she nor her mother really deserved the *osushi,* for they hadn't come up with a single good idea to help Mrs. K. But neither had Mr. Kitamura, and he got a small dish of *osushi* too. Mrs. K. had put it in front of his photograph that stood beside the black and gold altar with the small statue of Buddha and the incense and candle.

In fact, ever since he died years ago, Mr. Kitamura always got a small dish of anything good that Mrs. K. made, and Miyo wondered if he came down from the Pure Land in the middle of the night to eat it. Mrs. K. told her, however, that the food was for his spirit, and that it reached him just as her love and thoughts did, in a wonderful way that she couldn't quite explain.

"I do wish we could think of a way to help Mrs. K.," Mother said as they ate Mrs. K's delicious *osushi* and drank steaming cups of tea.

But Mother was so tired at the end of a long day looking after sick babies and children at the hospital that she just couldn't find any good ideas inside her head. She did say, however, that keeping Mr. Lincoln inside a carton in the house was not the answer.

And Mrs. K. certainly found out it wasn't. On the second night she brought him inside, Mr. Lincoln poked his way right out of the carton and walked all over her house. He scratched the floors and pecked at her sofa and got into a fight with Leonardo, the cat. By the time Mrs. K. got to them, there were feathers all over her living room and Leonardo almost had fresh chicken for breakfast.

"I suppose I will have to give Mr. Lincoln away," Mrs. K. murmured sadly. "But I can't give him to just anybody. It has to be someone who will love him and not turn him into fricassee or stew."

Mrs. K. lost three pounds from worrying and said she was becoming a nervous wreck. "If I can't find a new home for Mr. Lincoln, I suppose I will simply have to go to jail," she said, trying to look brave.

Miyo thought and thought until her jaws ached. How in the world could they find just the right person to take Mr. Lincoln? Then, suddenly, she had an idea.

"I know," she said brightly. "I'll put an ad in our class magazine."

Mrs. K. thought about it. "Well," she said slowly, "I suppose it won't do any harm."

What she really meant was that it probably wouldn't do any good either. But Miyo was determined to try. She had to hurry for Mrs. K. had already said several times that she was becoming a nervous wreck, and Miyo certainly didn't want her to stop being the nice, cheerful person she was.

Miyo's class magazine was almost ready to be mimeographed for the month of October. There were several sections, one each for news, feature stories, science, sports, book reviews, poetry, and, finally, a small section for ads. That's where Miyo thought Mr. Lincoln would fit nicely.

Wanted: Nice home for friendly, intelligent, dignified ROOSTER. P.S. He understands Japanese. Please hurry! Urgent! 555-4321

She made her ad very special. She wrote, "WANTED: NICE HOME FOR FRIENDLY, INTELLIGENT, DIGNIFIED ROOSTER. P.S. HE UNDERSTANDS JAPANESE." Then she added, "PLEASE HURRY! URGENT!"

Her teacher, Mrs. Fielding, told her it was a fine ad, and suggested that she include her phone number, so Miyo did. She also drew a picture of Mr. Lincoln beneath her ad, trying to make him look dignified and friendly.

The magazine came out on September 30. That very afternoon, a policeman rang the doorbell of Mrs. K's shaggy ivy-covered house.

"I've a complaint, Ma'am," he said,
"about a rooster?" He seemed to think there
might have been some mistake.

Mrs. K. sighed. "Come inside, officer,"
she said. "I've been expecting you." She
supposed now she would just have to go

quietly to jail, but first she wanted a cup of tea. "Would you like some tea?" she asked.

Officer McArdle was tired and his feet hurt. "Thank you, Ma'am," he said, and he came inside. He looked all around at Mrs. Kitamura's home, bulging with Japanese things he'd never seen before. There were Japanese dolls dancing inside dusty glass cases. There were scrolls of Japanese paintings hanging on the walls. There was the black and gold Buddhist altar, and spread out all over the dining room table were Japanese books and newspapers. Mrs. K. pushed them aside and put down a tray of tea and cookies.

"*Dozo,*" she said, "please have some tea." She took off her apron and smoothed down her frizzy gray hair. Then she told Officer McArdle all about her troubles with Mr. Lincoln.

He looked sympathetic, but he said, "You're breaking a city law by having a rooster in your yard. You really should be fined, you know."

Mrs. K. was astonished. "Even if I am only barely inside the city limits?"

Officer McArdle nodded. "I'm afraid so. I'll give you two more days to get rid of your rooster. Mr. Wickett says you're disturbing the peace."

Then he thanked her for the tea and cookies and he was gone.

Miyo was proud of the ad in her class magazine, but no one seemed at all interested in Mr. Lincoln. Instead, several people told her how much they liked her feature story about Mr. Botts, the school custodian, who was retiring.

She had written, "Say good-bye to the best custodian Hawthorn School ever had. Mr. Botts is retiring because he is getting tired. At the age of sixty-five, who wouldn't? He and Mrs. Botts are going to Far Creek. He is going to eat a lot and sleep a lot and maybe go fishing. So, so long, Mr. Botts. And good luck!"

Her teacher, Mrs. Fielding, told her it was a fine story.

On her way home, Miyo ran into Mr. Botts himself. He told her it was the first time in his entire life that anyone had written a feature story about him.

When he got home that night, he took off his shoes, sat in his favorite chair, lit a pipe, and read the magazine from cover to cover. At the bottom of page twenty, he saw Miyo's ad about Mr. Lincoln.

"Tami," he said to Mrs. Botts, who happened to be Japanese, "how would you like to have a rooster?"

"A what?"

"A rooster," Mr. Botts repeated. "One that understands Japanese."

Mrs. Botts thought that Mr. Botts had had too much excitement, what with his retirement party at school and all. But he kept right on talking.

"When we move to Far Creek, didn't you say you were going to grow vegetables and raise chickens while I go hunting and fishing?"

Mrs. Botts remembered having said something like that. "Yes, I guess I did."

"Well, if you're going to raise chickens, you'll need a rooster."

"Why, I guess that's so."

"Then we might as well have one that's friendly and dignified," Mr. Botts said, and he went right to the telephone to call Miyo.

"I'll take that rooster you want to find a home for," he said. "My wife, Tami, could talk to it in Japanese too."

Miyo couldn't believe it. Someone had actually read her ad and that someone was Mr. Botts and his wife. They would give Mr. Lincoln a fine home and surely wouldn't turn him into fricassee or stew. At last, she had done something to help Mrs. K. and keep her from becoming a nervous wreck. As soon as she told Mother, she ran right over to tell Mrs. K. the good news.

Mrs. K. was just about to stuff Mr. Lincoln into a wooden crate for the night. When Miyo told her that Mr. Lincoln would have a nice half-Japanese home in Far Creek with Mr. and Mrs. Botts, Mrs. K. gave Miyo such a hug she almost squeezed the breath out of her.

"Hooray! *Banzai!*" Mrs. K. said happily. "Tomorrow we will have a party to celebrate. I shall invite you and your mama, and Mr. and Mrs. Botts." And because Mrs. K. felt so relieved and happy, she even decided to invite Mr. Wickett.

263

"Even though you are a cross old man," she said to him, "I suppose you were right. A rooster shouldn't live in a small pen at the edge of town. He should live in the country where he'll have some hens to talk to and nobody will care if he crows at the sun."

Mr. Wickett was a little embarrassed to come to Mrs. K's party, but he was too

lonely to say no. He came with a box of chocolate-dipped cherries and said, "I'm sorry I caused such a commotion."

But Mrs. K. told him he needn't be sorry. "Life needs a little stirring up now and then," she admitted. "Besides," she added, "now both Mr. Lincoln and I have found new friends."

Miyo and her mother brought a caramel cake with Mr. Lincoln's initials on it and Mr. and Mrs. Botts brought Mrs. K. a philodendron plant. "Maybe you can talk to it in Japanese now instead of to Mr. Lincoln," Mrs. Botts said, "and don't worry, I'll take good care of him."

"You come on out to visit us and your rooster any time you like," Mr. Botts added.

Miyo's mother promised that one day soon she would drive them all up to Far Creek to see how Mr. Lincoln liked his new home.

When the party was over, Mr. Botts carried Mr. Lincoln in his crate to his station wagon. Mr. Lincoln gave a polite squawk of farewell and Mrs. K. promised she would come visit him soon.

"Good-bye, Mr. Lincoln. Good-bye, Mr. and Mrs. Botts," Miyo called.

From inside Mrs. K's kitchen, Hamilton, the parrot, screeched. "Good-bye, Mr. Lincoln. Good-bye."

Jefferson roused himself from his bed near the stove and came outside to wag his tail at everybody, and Leonardo rubbed up against Mrs. K's legs to remind her that he was still there.

Then Mr. Botts honked his horn and they were gone.

"I hope we'll see each other again soon," Mr. Wickett said to Mrs. K.

"Good night, Mr. Wickett," she answered. "I'm sure we will."

Miyo and her mother thanked Mrs. K. for the nice party and went home, leaving her to say good night to her potatoes and onions before going inside.

"Do you think she'll miss Mr. Lincoln a lot?" Miyo asked.

"She will for a while," Mother answered, "but now she has a new friend and neighbor to talk to."

Miyo nodded. That was true. And even if Mr. Wickett couldn't understand Japanese, at least he could answer back, and maybe that was even better than having an intelligent rooster around.

Miyo was glad everything had turned out so well, and went to bed feeling good inside.

"Good night, Mama," she called softly to her mother.

"Good night, Miyo," Mother answered as she tucked her in.

Then, one by one, the lights went out in all the houses along the street, and soon only the sounds of the insects filled the dark night air.

ALL THE ONES THEY CALL LOWLY

Garter snake, garter snake, you hurt no one;
You move on so gracefully through the grass.
Garter snake, garter snake, I'll be your friend
And not run away as you pass.

Grasshopper, grasshopper, hopping so high
Away from our crazy feet close to you;
Grasshopper, grasshopper, I'll be your friend;
I wish I could hop as high as you.

Speckled frog, speckled frog, I like your pad;
I don't believe I'll catch warts from you.
Speckled frog, speckled frog, I'll be your friend;
Why should I be frightened of you?

Wriggly worm, wriggly worm, get back inside—
A robin is waiting to take you home;
Wriggly worm, wriggly worm, I'll be your friend;
Above ground you'll not be alone.

All the ones that they do call lowly,
That do no harm to you or me—
Each will be my secret buddy
On grass and water, sand and tree.

David Campbell

Gone

by David McCord

I've looked behind the shed
And under every bed:
I think he must be dead.

What reason for alarm?
He doesn't know the farm.
I *knew* he'd come to harm!

He was a city one
Who never had begun
To think the city fun.

Now where could he have got?
He doesn't know a lot.
I haven't heard a shot.

That old abandoned well,
I thought. Perhaps he fell?
He didn't. I could tell.

Perhaps he found a scent:
A rabbit. Off he went.
He'll come back home all spent.

Groundhogs, they say, can fight;
And raccoons will at night.
He'd not know one by sight!

I've called and called his name.
I'll never be the same.
I blame myself . . . I blame . . .

All *he* knows is the park;
And now it's growing dark.
A bark? *You hear a bark?*

TURTLE KNOWS YOUR NAME

a folk tale from the West Indies

retold and illustrated by
Ashley Bryan

nce there was a little boy and he had a very long name.

His name was UPSILIMANA TUMPALERADO.

It was easy to pronounce, UP-SILI-MANA TUM-PA-LERADO, but it was hard to remember.

His grandmother raised him in her village by the sea.

She taught him to walk. She taught him to talk. But teaching him to walk and to talk wasn't the same as teaching him to say his name, uh-uh!

That took time, and Granny took her time. She said his name to him slowly:

"UP-SILI-MANA TUM-PA-LERADO."

"UPALA TUMPALO!" said the grandson.

"Uh-uh!" said Granny, shaking her head from side to side. "Uh-uh, uh-uh!"

She didn't give up, though.

"Turtle takes his time," she said. "I take mine, and you take your time, too."

And he did. Then one day he said it:

"UPSILIMANA TUMPALERADO!"

"Uh-huh!" cried the grandmother.

She was so happy, she hugged him once, she kissed him twice, she swung him around, wheee, three times! She shook his hand, then took his hand, and they ran down to the sandy beach.

"Here's where we dance your name dance," said Granny. "Sing your name, loud and clear. Sing it to me. Sing it to the sea!"

Granny clapped as they danced. Her grandson sang:

"UPSILIMANA TUMPALERADO,
That's my name.
I took my time to learn it,
Won't you do the same?"

Turtle, who lived nearby, heard the singing and swam closer. The villagers always came to the shore to sing and dance their children's names. Turtle loved to gather names, and he never missed a name dance. Turtle was older than anyone could tell. He even remembered Granny's name dance when Granny, as a little girl, danced with her granny on the shore. Turtle raised his head above the water and listened.

"UPSILIMANA TUMPALERADO, that's my name," sang the boy again and again.

"A long name," said Turtle. "But a good song name to dance to. I think I've got it."

Turtle flipped and dove to the bottom of the sea. In his coral home, Turtle smoothed a space and spelled the name with shells. He blinked and said:

"UPSILIMANA TUMPALERADO, uh-huh! I know it well."

Now that her grandson knew it well, too, Granny let him go out alone to play in the village. Each time he set out to play, she'd say:

"UPSILIMANA TUMPALERADO, teach your name to your playmates and do your best. Remember, your name is long, but it's not the longest."

UPSILIMANA TUMPALERADO always had a good time playing with the village children. He learned their names quickly: Zamba, Mogans, Dandoo, Brashee . . . and he remembered them. He taught them his name, too. But no one ever remembered it.

"Ho, Long Name!" they'd call. "Your turn to hide the stick."

"My name is not Long Name," he'd say. "My name is UPSILIMANA TUMPALERADO."

"Uh-huh," they'd say. "But it's still your turn, Long Name."

His name *was* always the longest. What, then, did Granny mean when she'd say, "Your name is long, but it's not the longest"?

One morning UPSILIMANA TUMPALERADO said, "Granny, I'm not going to be called Long Name today. I'm going to play with the animals."

"Don't be late for dinner," said Granny. "I'm cooking fungi."

"Fungi!" exclaimed the boy.

"Uh-huh!" said Granny. "If you're late, I might be tempted to eat all the fungi myself."

"Uh-uh!" said the boy. "I won't be late! You'll see. Bye, Granny. Twee-twaa-twee."

Off he went, whistling twee-twaa-twee, twee-twaa-twee.

He came to a field and saw a donkey rubbing its hide against a tree. The boy sang:

> *"Donkey, hee, donkey, oh!*
> *My name is UPSILIMANA TUMPALERADO.*
> *Shall I call it out once more?"*

The donkey brayed, "Haw, hee-haw," and rubbed its hide just as before.

"Well, twee-twaa-twee," whistled the boy, and he ran across the field. He clambered up on the rocks bordering the field. There he met a goat bounding from stone to stone. The boy sang:

"Goat, hah, goat, oh!
My name is UPSILIMANA TUMPALERADO.
Say it loud. Say it clear."

The goat bleated, "Bleah, bleah-bleah," and leaped
as if it didn't care.

"Well, twee-twaa-twee," whistled the boy. He
jumped from the rocks into the pasture near the
seashore. There he saw a cow. The boy sang:

"Cow, ho, cow, oh!
My name is UPSILIMANA TUMPALERADO.
Say it, and I'll dance for you."

The cow lowed, "Moo, moo-moo," then mooed
once more and stopped to chew.

"Well, twee-twaa-twee," whistled the boy. He spun
around swiftly and bumped into a pig.

"Oh, pardon, pig," he said. "My name is . . ." and
he stopped short.

"Uh-uh! I won't tell you my name. You'll do the
same as the others."

He ran past pig in the pasture, past pawpaw and palm trees till he came to the beach.

He splashed in the sea, whistling, "Twee-twaa-twee."

Turtle heard the splashing. He swam up to the boy and said:

> "*UPSILIMANA TUMPALERADO,*
> *I'm so glad you came.*
> *UPSILIMANA TUMPALERADO,*
> *Turtle knows your name.*"

The boy slapped the water for joy, splish-splash, splish-splash!

"Turtle, oh, Turtle," he cried. "How did you know that my name is UPSILIMANA TUMPALERADO?"

Turtle didn't stay to play or answer questions. He dove under the waves and disappeared.

The boy called and called till his stomach ached, but Turtle did not return.

"I've yelled myself hoarse, hollow, and hungry," he said to himself. "The fungi, oh, the fungi!"

He ran as fast as he could go. He ran past pawpaw and palm trees, past pig in the pasture, past cow who gazed, grazed, and mooed, past goat bounding high over the rocks, bleah-bleah, past donkey in the field, hee-haw, hee-haw. He ran into his house, crying:

"Granny! Granny! Please, I'm hungry. The fungi, the fungi!"

With her large wooden spoon, Granny was turning the cornmeal in the pot. She smiled at her grandson as she ladled some into a buttered bowl and shook it till it was round as a grapefruit. She rolled it onto her grandson's plate of fish.

"Thank you, Granny. Fungi rolled in a bowl till it's round as a ball and as yellow as gold is the best of all."

"Sing it!" said Granny. She hummed as she shook a bowl of fungi for herself:

"Fungi rolled in a bowl
Till it's round as a ball
And as yellow as gold
Is the best of all."

They finished eating the fungi and fish. Then Granny set a plate of bread pudding and a sweet-potato pie on the table.

"He who asks, don't get. He who don't ask, don't want," said Granny.

Granny always said that before offering dessert. She'd laugh as she watched the puzzled look on her grandson's face. Then she'd offer him a way out.

"Tell me a proverb," she'd say, "and I'll give you dessert."

"A proverb? No problem!" UPSILIMANA TUMPALERADO would say. He had learned lots of proverbs.

He'd answer with: "A man can't grow taller than his head" or "You'll never catch a black cat at night." His favorite was "If a baboon wants to whistle, don't stop him."

But this time, Granny didn't ask for a proverb.

Instead she said, "Tell me my name, UPSILIMANA TUMPALERADO."

"Oh, Granny, that's easier than a proverb," said the boy. "Your name is Granny!"

He laughed and passed his plate.

"Uh-uh," said Granny. "There are grannies all over the village. Every granny has a name. Tell me mine, or no dessert."

Granny took a bite of her bread pudding. UPSILIMANA TUMPALERADO looked at Granny. She licked her lips and rolled her eyes. He looked longingly at the dessert.

"I will find out your real name, Granny," he said. "Then I will have dessert, too."

UPSILIMANA TUMPALERADO jumped up from the table and ran off to the village. He stopped the villagers and asked:

"Do you know my granny's name?
Will you tell it to me plain?
I won't get bread pudding
Or sweet-potato pie
Until I tell her real name to her;
Saying 'Granny' just won't do her."

The villagers circled him and sang:

"Grass, plants, bees, bells,
Sky, birds, seas, shells,
Guava, plantain, mango trees—
Call them anything you please.
They will always be the same
'Cause Granny is your granny's name."

The villagers danced as they sang the song over and over. Drummers picked up the beat. For a while, UPSILIMANA TUMPALERADO forgot his question and danced quick steps to match the best of the dancers. Then he remembered.

"This won't get me dessert," he said to himself.

He could hear the villagers still chanting, "Granny is your granny's name," as he hurried away to the animals.

He ran to the donkey, haw, hee-haw. Donkey wouldn't help him, didn't want to. Goat and cow were just the same, wouldn't help him with the name, bleah-bleah, moo-moo.

Perhaps Turtle would help. Turtle knew his name. Turtle had said his name before. He kept on running till he reached the shore.

He called till Turtle swam up from his coral home at the bottom of the sea. Then the boy sang:

"Turtle, tell me Granny's name.
Will you tell it to me plain?
I won't get bread pudding
Or sweet-potato pie
Until I tell her real name to her;
Saying 'Granny' just won't do her."

Turtle listened to the sweet, sad song. Then Turtle sang:

"UPSILIMANA TUMPALERADO,
Turtle knows your name.
Gathering names is what I do.
I know Granny's real name, too."

"Oh, teach me, Turtle, teach me!" cried the boy.

"First, promise not to tell who told you," said Turtle.

The boy promised and Turtle taught him his granny's name.

"Uh-huh! So that's why Granny always says to me, 'Your name is long, but it's not the longest.'"

He thanked Turtle and ran home.

"Dessert, please, dessert!" cried the boy as he ran into the room.

"Well, UPSILIMANA TUMPALERADO, first tell me my real name."

"Your name is MAPASEEDO JACKALINDY EYE PIE TACKARINDY!"

"Why, UPSILIMANA TUMPALERADO, that's right, uh-huh!"

She served her grandson a large square of bread pudding.

"Tell me, UPSILIMANA TUMPALERADO, who told you my name?"

"Oh, MAPASEEDO JACKALINDY EYE PIE TACKARINDY, I can't tell you."

"Why can't you tell me, UPSILIMANA TUMPALERADO?"

"I promised not to, MAPASEEDO JACKALINDY EYE PIE TACKARINDY."

"Well, then, UPSILIMANA TUMPALERADO, I'll find out for myself."

Granny put on her large straw hat and went into the village. She stopped in the marketplace and said to the villagers:

"My grandson came
And asked my name.
Did you tell it?
Who can spell it?"

The villagers clapped and sang:

"Long Name came
And asked your name.
So we told him, and it's true,
Granny is our name for you."

"That's not the name my grandson told me," said Granny, and off she went.

Granny's search for an answer took her across the field, over the rocks, through the pasture. She asked the same question of all the animals she met along the way. Donkey bawled, "Haw, hee-haw." Goat bleated, "Bleah, bleah-bleah." Cow answered, "Moo, moo-moo." None of that would do.

At last Granny came to the beach. Turtle was sunning himself on the sand, out of reach of the waves. She sat down beside him and asked:

"Turtle, did you teach my name?
My grandson says it well.
Were you the one who made him promise
Not to tell?"

Turtle answered:

"Yes, I taught your grandson
To say your name.
I thought it was the thing to do.
And now, I'll tell it to you, too.
It's MAPASEEDO JACKALINDY EYE PIE
    TACKARINDY."

Granny leaped up and spun with the news.

"How did you remember my long, long name from so long ago?" asked Granny.

Turtle answered:

"I learn names from the beach name dances.
I remember them well, because I take no chances.
I swim up and listen, though you don't see me.
Then I spell your names in shells at the bottom of
    the sea."

Turtle rose up on his short legs and waddled to the water. With a swish, swoosh, he slipped into the sea.

Granny waved as Turtle swam out. He dove and disappeared as Granny sang:

"Turtle knows your name, uh-huh!
Turtle knows your name."

When Granny reached home, her grandson stood at the door with an empty plate. He'd eaten all the bread pudding.

"Oh, MAPASEEDO JACKALINDY EYE PIE TACKARINDY," he said, "now for some sweet-potato pie."

"Aha, UPSILIMANA TUMPALERADO," said MAPASEEDO JACKALINDY EYE PIE TACKARINDY, "I know who knows our names."

They smiled at each other and called out together:

"Turtle knows your name!"

Then MAPASEEDO JACKALINDY EYE PIE TACKARINDY hugged UPSILIMANA TUMPALERADO and cut two slices of sweet-potato pie.

"Thank you, MAPASEEDO JACKALINDY EYE PIE TACKARINDY," said UPSILIMANA TUMPALERADO. "I love your pudding. I love your sweet-potato pie."

"Well, good, UPSILIMANA TUMPALERADO," said MAPASEEDO JACKALINDY EYE PIE TACKARINDY. "You can thank Turtle for dessert."

"Uh-huh, MAPASEEDO JACKA . . ."

But before he could finish saying her name, Granny clapped her hand over her grandson's mouth.

"Listen," she said, "promise not to tell anyone else my name. And from now on, just call me 'Granny' and nothing more. Call me 'Granny,' the way you did before."

UPSILIMANA TUMPALERADO shook his head, and Granny took her hand from his mouth.

"Uh-huh, Granny!" he said.

"And furthermore," said Granny, "from now on, I'm going to call you 'Son.'"

They burst out laughing and finished the pie.

"Mmm . . . I love you, Granny!"

"Mmmm . . . mmm . . . I love you, Son!"

meet Ashley

Ashley Bryan learned at an early age to use his drawing talent. In kindergarten, he created his first books, which were *A-B-C* and counting books.

Bryan's childhood was filled with music. Sweet sounds came from his father's saxophone, guitar, and banjo. His mother sang often, and so did the many birds in the family's apartment.

The artist's drawings of animals and people dance across the pages of the African and Caribbean folk tales he retells. Bryan splashes *Turtle Knows Your Name* with colorful paintings. In other books, he uses

Woodcut illustration from
Lion and the Ostrich Chicks

296

Bryan

Woodcut illustration from
Beat the Story Drum, Pum-Pum

bold woodcuts or lively line drawings. Bryan's storytelling and drawings come both from his African heritage and from everyday life. He says about his writing, "I play with sounds and I encourage others to read my stories aloud."

Perhaps the turtle in *Turtle Knows Your Name* also knows Ashley Bryan's name. Of course, many people do know and respect the name of Ashley Bryan. In fact, some of these people gave him the Coretta Scott King Award for his book *Beat the Story Drum, Pum-Pum.*

Line drawing from
The Dancing Granny

Woodcut illustration from
Walk Together Children

HURT NO LIVING THING

Hurt no living thing,
Ladybird nor butterfly,
Nor moth with dusty wing,
Nor cricket chirping cheerily,
Nor grasshopper, so light of leap,
Nor dancing gnat,
Nor beetle fat,
Nor harmless worms that creep.

Christina Rossetti

Tropical Forest with Monkeys
by Henri Rousseau

298

Reading Resources

CONTENTS

Find it, buy it, sell it, or what___r! To place your ad i___
Downtown Gazette Classified___ all Ms. Melendez,

HELP WANTED
___tent for downtown
___ manner,
___
___

PETS FOR A___
Our dog___
(our baby___
year-old___
playful.___
Myra ___

___able dog walker av___ et me
___ your pet get neede___ ___ger
an___ ___aring and resp___
Call J___

___St. A___ ___s
___ ___nder 12___ ___s
___dults. Refre___ ___x
___eds to ben___ the F___
___laygrounds___ ___furthe___
___ation, call 5___ ___8937.

___ur Spring Cleaning! Come
___sure! Furniture, antiques,
___all appliances, clothing,
___ay April 19, 10 AM—
___ Sunday April 26).

Desert Ecosystem
__ng things get the energy they need __ to survive in different ways.

Scavengers get their energy by eating dead animals or insects. A turkey vulture flies overhead, looking for dead animals.

Producers use the sun's energy, along with substances ___als to ___er.

Charts and Tables

SOME OF OUR NATIONAL PARKS

THE UNITED STATES HAS 50 NATIONAL PARKS.

NAME	LOCATION	YEAR(S) ESTABLISHED	RANK IN SIZE	SPECIAL FEATURES
Badlands	South Dakota	1929–1978	25	bison, bighorn sheep, antelope, fossil animals 40 million years old
Channel Islands	California	1938–1980	24	sea lion breeding grounds, nesting sea birds, unusual plants
Everglades	Florida	1934	9	largest remaining subtropical wilderness in continental U.S.
Grand Canyon	Arizona	1908–1919	10	most spectacular part of Colorado River canyon
Great Smoky Mountains	North Carolina and Tennessee	1926–1934	17	largest mountain range in eastern U.S., magnificent forests
Kenai Fjords	Alaska	1978–1980	15	mountain goats, marine mammals, bird life, large icecap
Olympic	Washington	1909–1938	12	mountain wilderness with finest remaining rain forest of Pacific Northwest
Redwood	California	1968	34	Pacific coastline, groves of ancient redwoods, world's tallest trees
Samoa	American Samoa	1988	49	tropical rain forest
Yellowstone	Idaho, Wyoming, Montana	1872	7	geysers, hot springs, canyons waterfalls, grizzly bear, moose, bison

SOME RARE ANIMALS

NAME OF ANIMAL (KIND)	NUMBER IN WILD (ESTIMATED)	NUMBER IN ZOOS	YOUNG BORN IN ZOOS (1 YEAR)
Cougar (Florida)	30	2	0
Elephant (Asian)	X	238	1
Gorilla (mountain)	400	1	X
Leopard (snow)	1,000	292	27
Lion (Asiatic)	250	196	0
Rhinoceros (black)	3,500	130	5
Anteater	X	107	4
Bear (polar)	10,000	200	6
Jaguar	X	202	12
Panda (giant)	1,000	17	0
Condor (California)	0	68	0
Parrot (golden-shouldered)	250	22	9
Boa (Puerto Rican)	X	63	14
Crocodile (Cuban)	1,000	83	1
Frog (Goliath)	X	3	X

x= not known

Diagrams

A WEATHER STATION

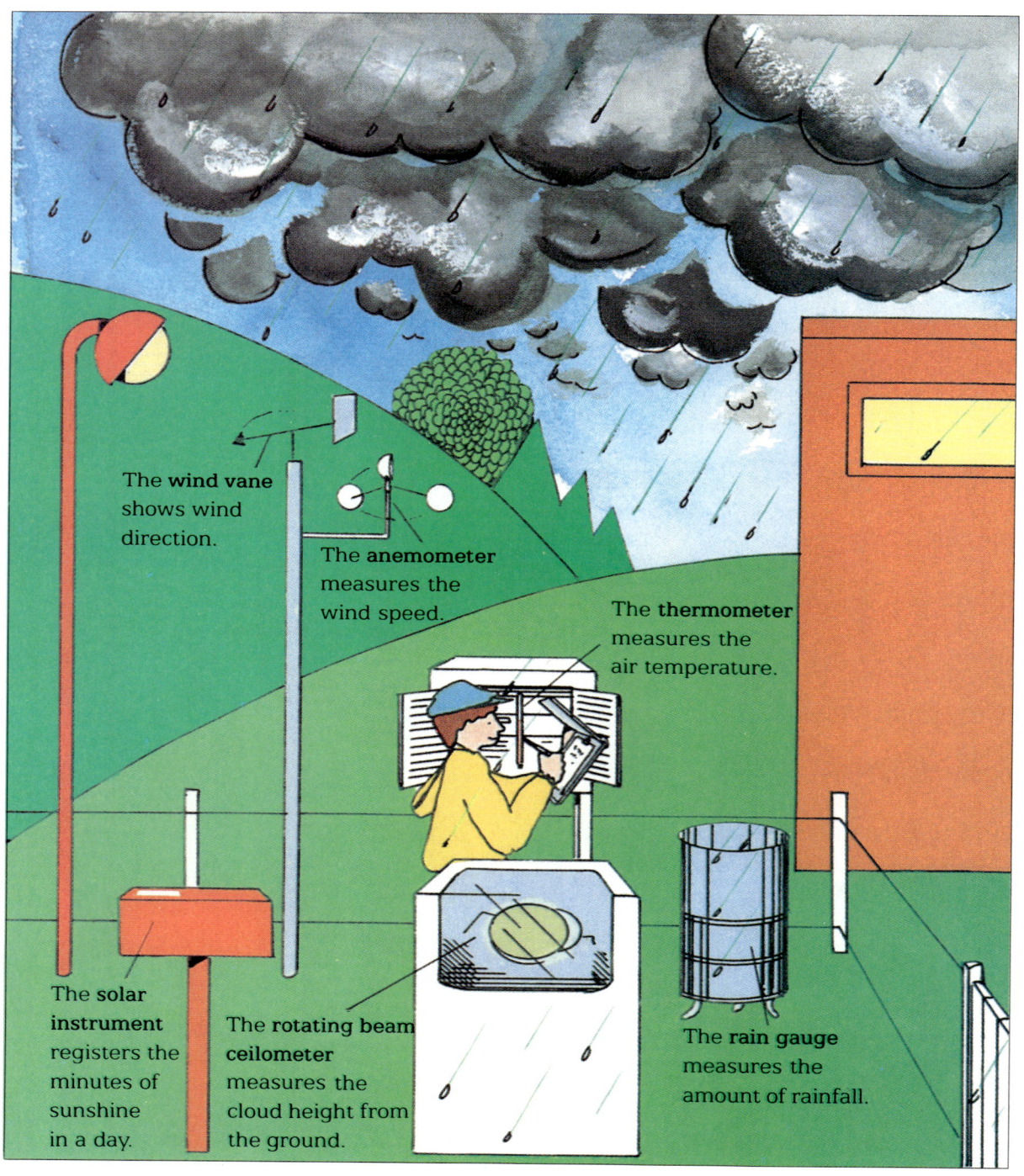

The **wind vane** shows wind direction.

The **anemometer** measures the wind speed.

The **thermometer** measures the air temperature.

The **solar instrument** registers the minutes of sunshine in a day.

The **rotating beam ceilometer** measures the cloud height from the ground.

The **rain gauge** measures the amount of rainfall.

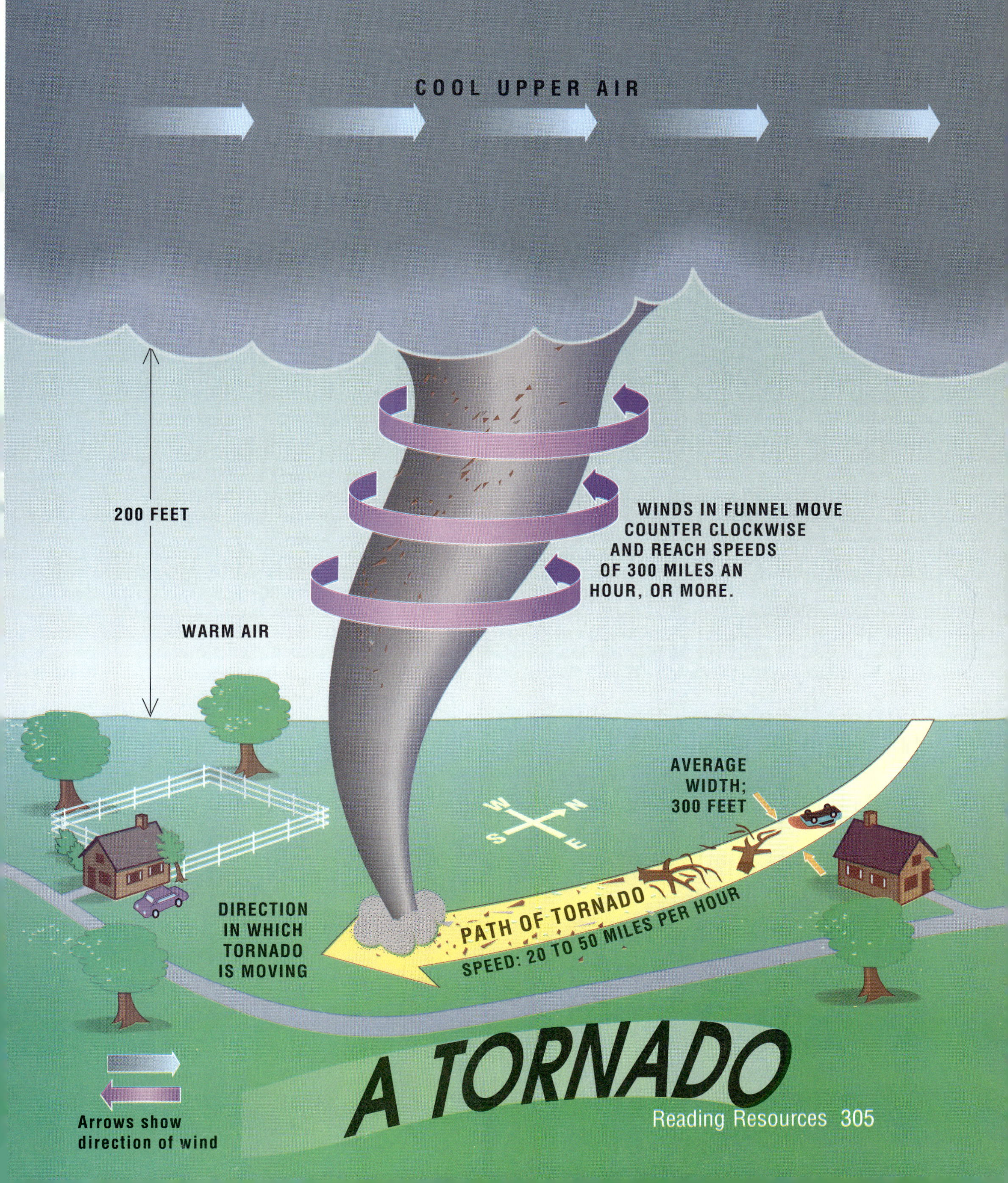

COOL UPPER AIR

200 FEET

WARM AIR

WINDS IN FUNNEL MOVE
COUNTER CLOCKWISE
AND REACH SPEEDS
OF 300 MILES AN
HOUR, OR MORE.

AVERAGE
WIDTH;
300 FEET

N
W E
S

DIRECTION
IN WHICH
TORNADO
IS MOVING

PATH OF TORNADO
SPEED: 20 TO 50 MILES PER HOUR

A TORNADO

Arrows show
direction of wind

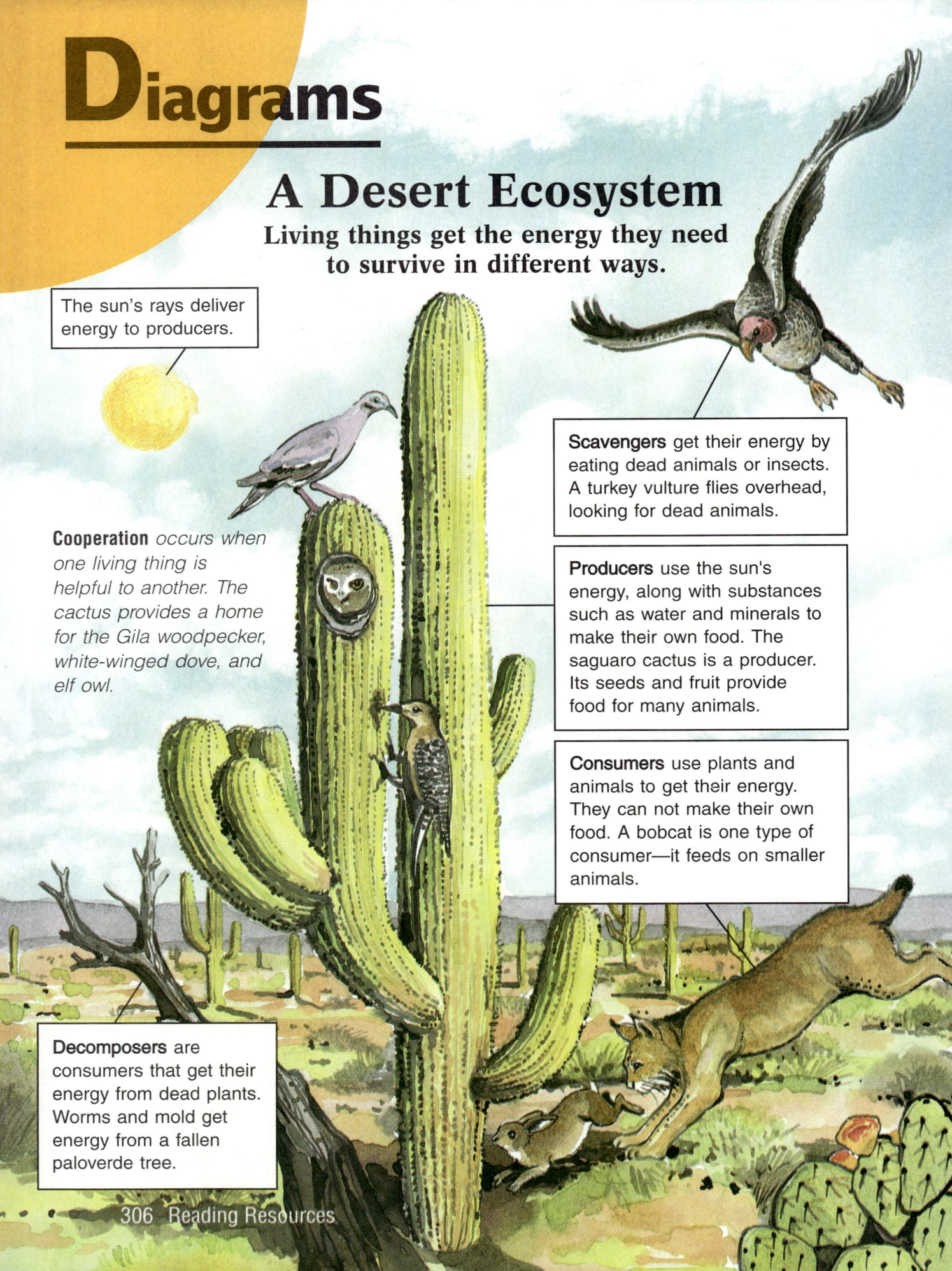

Diagrams

A Desert Ecosystem
Living things get the energy they need to survive in different ways.

The sun's rays deliver energy to producers.

Cooperation *occurs when one living thing is helpful to another. The cactus provides a home for the Gila woodpecker, white-winged dove, and elf owl.*

Scavengers get their energy by eating dead animals or insects. A turkey vulture flies overhead, looking for dead animals.

Producers use the sun's energy, along with substances such as water and minerals to make their own food. The saguaro cactus is a producer. Its seeds and fruit provide food for many animals.

Consumers use plants and animals to get their energy. They can not make their own food. A bobcat is one type of consumer—it feeds on smaller animals.

Decomposers are consumers that get their energy from dead plants. Worms and mold get energy from a fallen paloverde tree.

Forms and Applications

You're sure to enjoy these fine folk collections from
WORLDWIDE MUSIC INTERNATIONAL.
Our collections of authentic world folk music are now available on CD!

CALL TOLL FREE 800-555-5555
FOR YOUR CREDIT CARD ORDER, OR USE THE FORM BELOW.

Detach Here --- *Detach Here*

ORDER FORM

Collection Title	Order #	CD Price
Celtic Songs and Fiddle Tunes	1945	$14.95
Roots of Rap	1835	$12.95
Roots of Rock	1821	$12.95
Roots of Reggae	1811	$12.95
Folk Songs of the Americas	1918	$11.95
Israeli Folk Tunes	1903	$14.95
Music of African Peoples	1959	$14.95
Music of Indonesia	1981	$10.95
Percussion Music from Around the World	1991	$14.95

PLEASE PRINT

Claire Norman
Name

141 Third Street   Tulsa   OK
Address   City   State

00000   000-555-8875
Zip   Phone

ITEM #	QTY.	TITLE	ITEM PRICE	TOTAL
1945	1	Celtic Songs and Fiddle Tunes	14.95	14.95
1959	1	Music of African Peoples	14.95	14.95

PAYMENT METHOD (Check One)

☑ Check   ☐ Money Order   ☐ Credit Card

Account Number _____   Expiration Date _____

TOTAL ITEM CHARGES	29.90
POSTAGE ($.50 per item)	1.00
PRICE AND POSTAGE TOTAL	30.90
2-DAY RUSH DELIVERY ($9.95)	
TAX (5% for Iowa residents)	
TOTAL	30.90

MAIL ORDERS TO: Worldwide Music International,
P.O. Box 1010, Chanticlere, IA 00000

ALLOW 3–4 WEEKS FOR DELIVERY

Graphs

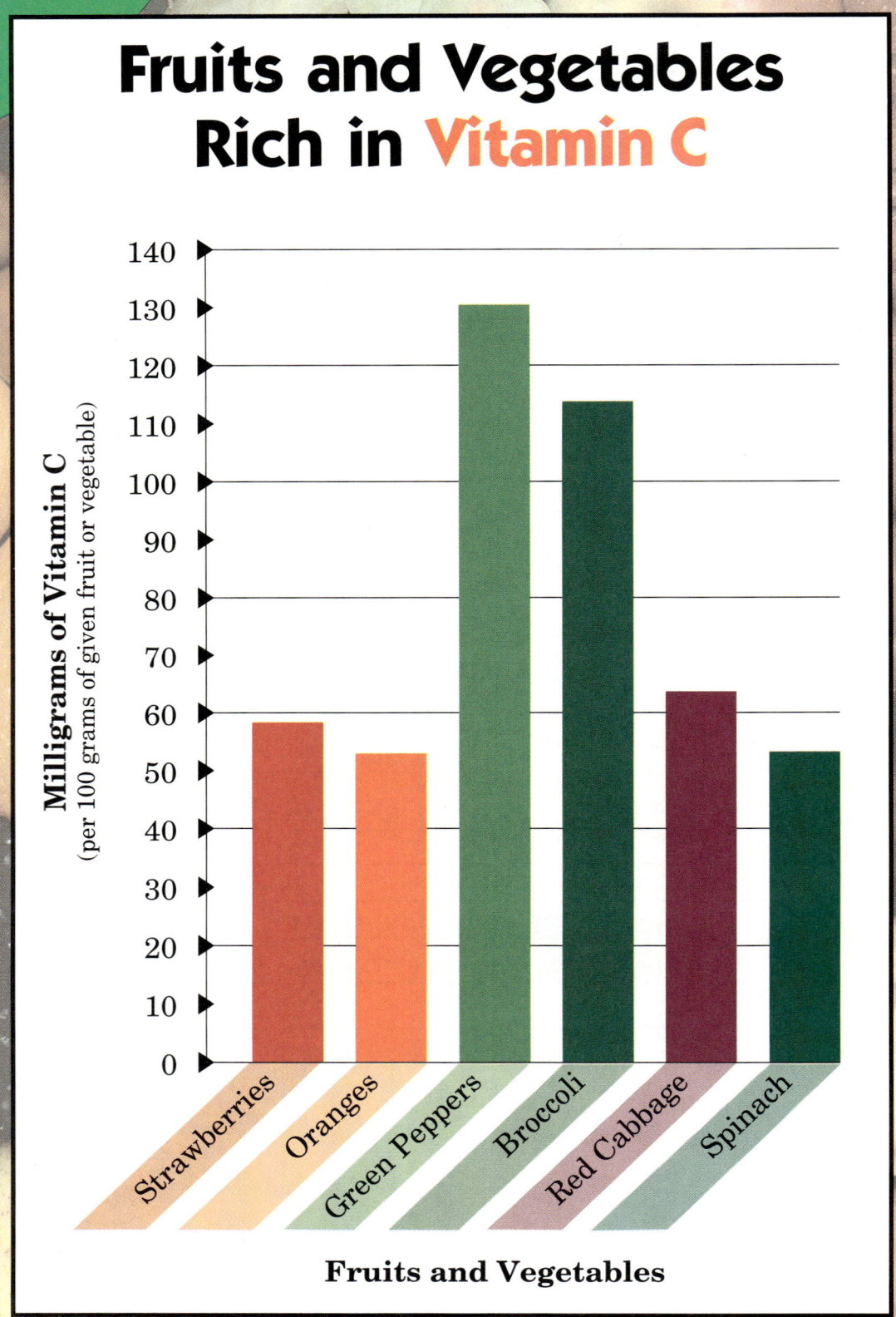

Fruits and Vegetables Rich in Vitamin C

Milligrams of Vitamin C
(per 100 grams of given fruit or vegetable)

140
130
120
110
100
90
80
70
60
50
40
30
20
10
0

Strawberries
Oranges
Green Peppers
Broccoli
Red Cabbage
Spinach

Fruits and Vegetables

GRAPHS

Area of Selected Crops Grown in the United States

CROP	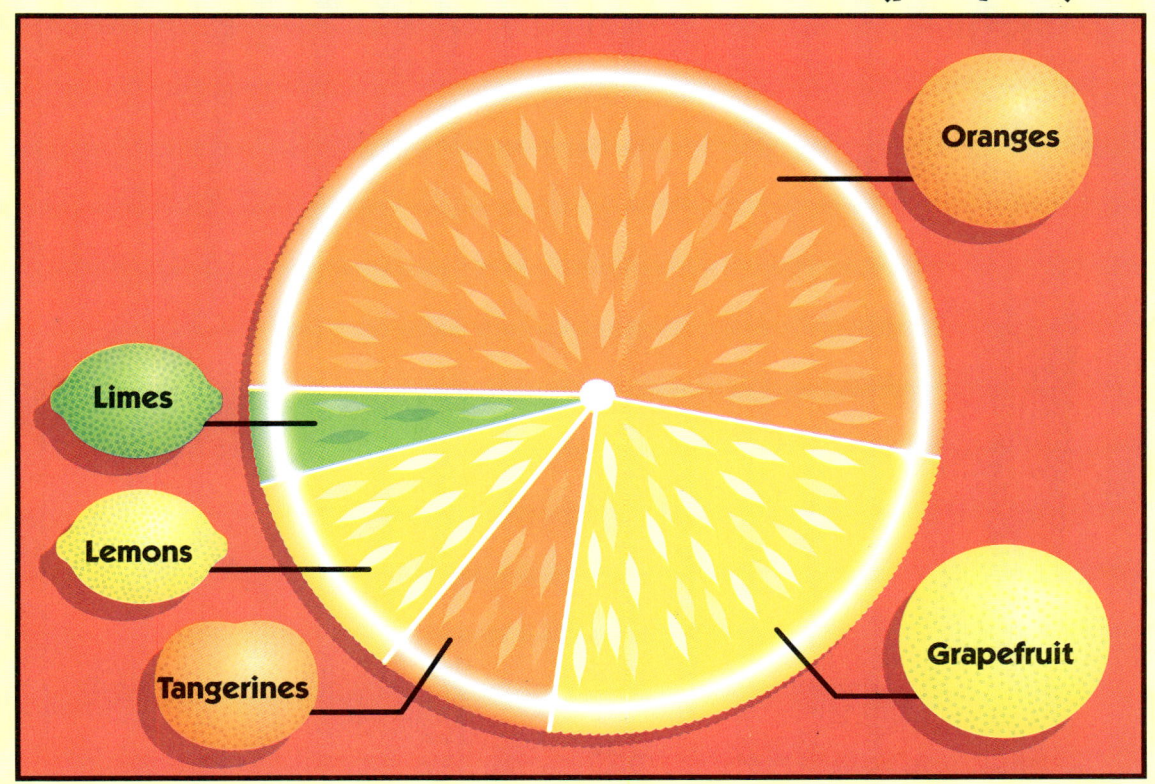 = 25,000 acres
Asparagus 🥬	🏠🏠🏠🏠
Broccoli 🥦	🏠🏠🏠🏠🏠
Carrots 🥕	🏠🏠🏠🏠🏠
Honeydew Melons 🍈	🏠
Lettuce 🥬	🏠🏠🏠🏠🏠🏠🏠🏠
Strawberries 🍓	🏠🏠
Sweet Potatoes 🥔	🏠🏠🏠
Tomatoes 🍅	🏠🏠🏠🏠🏠🏠🏠🏠🏠🏠🏠🏠🏠🏠🏠🏠🏠🏠🏠🏠🏠

Citus Fruit Eaten in the United States (per year)

Limes
Oranges
Lemons
Tangerines
Grapefruit

Maps

CENTRAL LIBRARY   FIRST FLOOR

Education and
Job Center

Meeting
Room

Languages,
Literature,
and Fiction

Children's Room

KEY

?	Information Desk
	Men's Room
	Women's Room
	Handicap Access
	Check out/ Library Cards
	Telephone
	Returns
	Card Catalog
	Computerized Catalog
	Photocopier
	Elevator
	Stairs

Videos

Art and Music

Periodicals

History and Biography

Maps

ARCTIC OCEAN

Eskimo

Ingalik

Aleut

Han

Kaska

Tlingit

Haida

Chipewyan

Kwakiutl

Nootka

Kutenai

Blackfoot

Chinook Yakima Flathead

Nez Percé

Klamath

Modoc Paiute

Pomo

Shoshone

Yokuts Ute

Paiute

Hopi Navajo

Zuni Pueblo

Pima

Papago

Apache

Concho

Yaqui

Coahuiltec

Eskimo

Hudson Bay

Eskimo

Naskapi

Cree

Micmac
Penobscot

Objibwa

Great
Lakes Ottawa

Sioux

Hidatsa

Cheyenne

Pawnee

Arapaho

Kansa

Sauk
Fox
Kickapoo
Winnebagos

Potwatami

Miami

Iroquois Narraganset
Wampanoag

Delaware

Kiowa Osage

Comanche Wichita

Caddo

Shawnee
Chickasaw

Choctaw

Cherokee

Creek

Timucuan

Gulf of Mexico

Taino

Ciboney

Caribbean Sea

Aztec
Mixtec
Zapotec

Maya

Mosquito

PACIFIC
OCEAN

ATLANTIC
OCEAN

0   250   500 Miles

0 250 500 750 Kilometers

INDIAN GROUPS OF NORTH AMERICA

- Arctic
- Subarctic
- Northwest Coast
- California
- Basin and Plateau
- Southwest
- Plains
- Eastern Woodlands
- Middle America
- Caribbean
- Northern Mexico

N

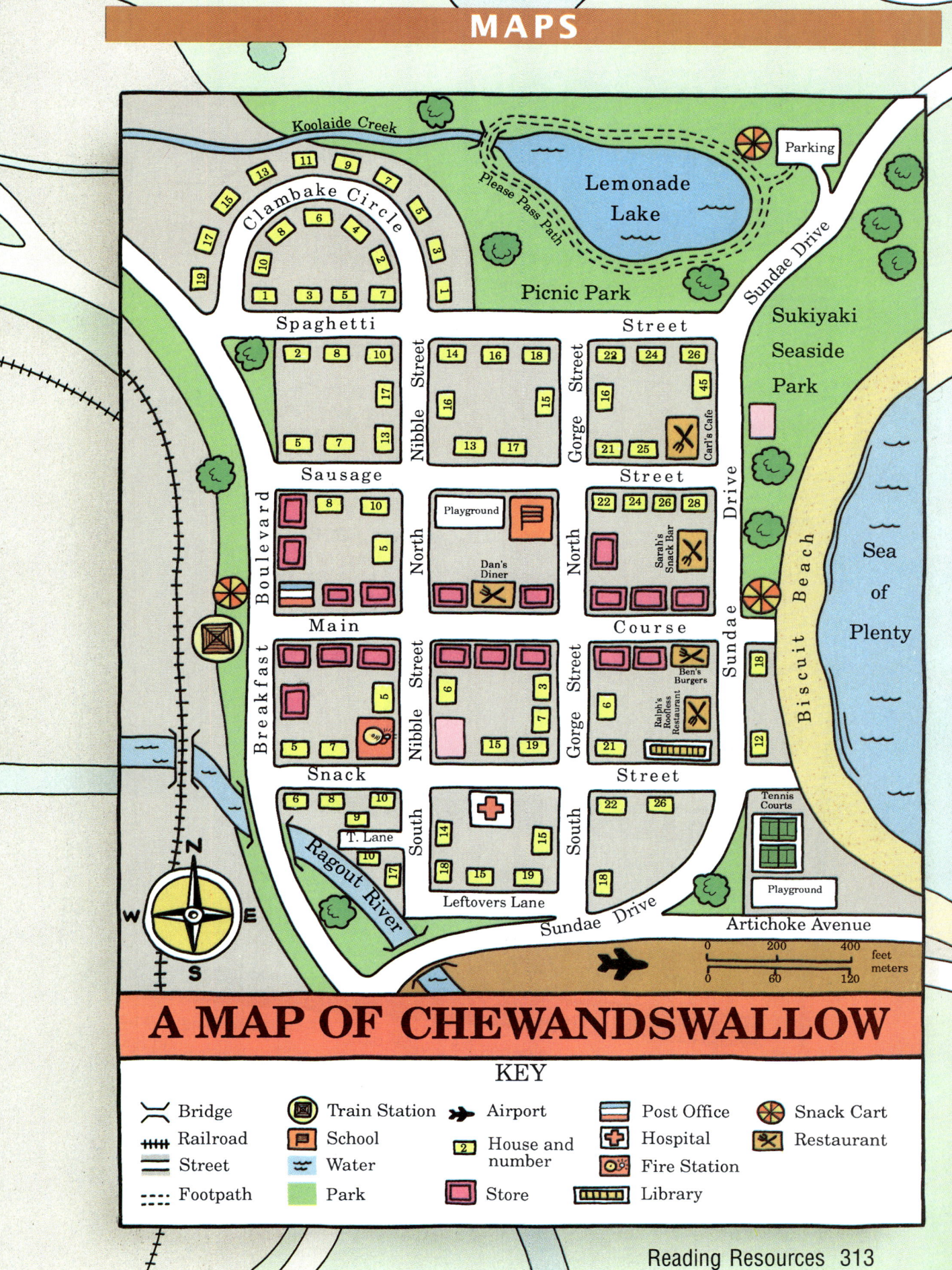

A MAP OF CHEWANDSWALLOW

KEY

- ⨝ Bridge
- ⊞⊞ Railroad
- ☰ Street
- ···· Footpath
- ⊚ Train Station
- ⊡ School
- ≈ Water
- Park
- ✈ Airport
- 2 House and number
- ▭ Store
- Post Office
- ✚ Hospital
- Fire Station
- Library
- Snack Cart
- ✗ Restaurant

Newspapers

—DOWNTOWN GAZETTE—
CLASSIFIEDS

Find it, buy it, sell it, or whatever! To place your ad in the *Downtown Gazette* Classifieds, call Ms. Melendez, 555-8000.

HELP WANTED

Office Assistant for downtown business. Good phone manner, word processing skills nec. Flexible hours. Call Ms. Bellis 555-7124.

Newspaper Delivery—Deliver the *Downtown Gazette!* Routes open in North End and Old Town. Ideal for students. Call Mr. Margolies 555-5827.

Services Available

No Job Too Small! Painting, carpentry, general handywork. Reasonable rates. Call for free estimates. Maggie 555-4025.

Reliable dog walker available. Let me help your pet get needed exercise. I am a caring and responsible teenager who loves dogs. References available. Call Josh 555-4382.

PETS FOR ADOPTION

Our dog, Max, needs a new home (our baby has allergies). He is a 6-year-old cocker/poodle mix, healthy, playful, affectionate. Call Jason or Myra 555-8099.

AKC-registered German shepherd puppies. $50. Call after 6 PM. 555-1296.

EVENTS

Want to celebrate the good weather? Need to sing and stomp your feet? Take the family to an outdoor Children's Concert, Sunday April 19, 4 PM (rain or shine!). In the large yard at Community Hall, 434 Main St. Admission $1 for children under 12, $2 for teenagers and adults. Refreshments available. Proceeds to benefit the Fund to Fix Our Playgrounds. For further information, call 555-8937.

TAG SALES

Large variety of children's goods for sale—clothing, toys, books. Saturday April 18, 10 AM–6 PM (raindate Sunday April 19). 85 Elm St.

We did our Spring Cleaning! Come find a treasure! Furniture, antiques, bicycles, small appliances, clothing, dishes. Sunday April 19, 10 AM–5 PM (raindate Sunday April 26). 14 Mountain Ave.

Schedules

Sundays/Holidays*

SAN FRANCISCO TO SAN JOSE

			TRAIN NO. — AM		TRAIN NO. — PM						
			92	**40**	**44**	**48**	**94**	**98**	**76**	**78**	**80**
MILES / ZONE / STATION											
0.0		Lv San Francisco @ 4th & Townsend Sts.	8:00	10:00	Noon	2:00	4:00	6:00	7:15	8:00	10:00
1.9	SF	Lv 22nd Street	8:05	10:05	12:05	2:05	4:05	6:05	7:20	8:05	10:05
4.1		Lv Paul Avenue	8:09	—	—	—	4:09	6:09	—	—	—
5.2		Lv Bayshore	8:12	10:10	12:10	2:10	4:12	6:12	7:25	8:10	10:10
9.3		Lv So. San Francisco	8:17	10:15	12:15	2:15	4:17	6:17	7:30	8:15	10:15
11.6	1	Lv San Bruno	8:21	10:19	12:19	2:19	4:21	6:21	7:34	8:19	10:19
13.7		Lv Millbrae	8:25	10:23	12:23	2:23	4:25	6:25	7:38	8:23	10:23
15.2		Lv Broadway	8:28	10:26	12:26	2:26	4:28	6:28	7:41	8:26	10:26
16.3		Lv Burlingame	8:31	10:28	12:28	2:28	4:30	6:30	7:44	8:28	10:28
17.9	2	Lv San Mateo	8:34	10:31	12:31	2:31	4:33	6:33	7:47	8:31	10:31
18.9		Lv Hayward Park	8:36	10:34	12:34	2:34	4:36	6:36	7:50	8:34	10:34
20.0		Lv Bay Meadows ●	—	—	—	—	—	—	—	—	—
20.3		Lv Hillsdale	8:39	10:37	12:37	2:37	4:39	6:39	7:53	8:37	10:37
21.9		Lv Belmont	8:42	10:40	12:40	2:40	4:42	6:42	7:56	8:40	10:40
23.2	3	Lv San Carlos	8:45	10:43	12:43	2:43	4:45	6:45	7:59	8:43	10:43
25.4		Lv Redwood City	8:49	10:47	12:47	2:47	4:49	6:49	8:03	8:47	10:47
27.8		Lv Atherton	8:53	10:51	12:51	2:51	4:53	6:53	8:07	8:51	10:51
28.9		Lv Menlo Park	8:56	10:53	12:53	2:53	4:55	6:55	8:10	8:53	10:53
30.1		Lv Palo Alto	8:59	10:56	12:56	2:56	4:58	6:58	8:13	8:56	10:56
31.8	4	Lv Stanford Stadium ●	—	—	—	—	—	—	—	—	—
34.8		Lv California Avenue	9:02	10:59	12:59	2:59	5:01	7:01	8:16	8:59	10:59
36.1		Lv Mountain View	9:08	11:05	1:05	3:05	5:07	7:07	8:22	9:05	11:05
38.8		Lv Sunnyvale	9:12	11:09	1:09	3:09	5:11	7:11	8:26	9:09	11:09
40.8	5	Lv Lawrence	9:16	11:12	1:12	3:12	5:15	7:15	8:30	9:12	11:12
44.3		Lv Santa Clara	9:20	11:17	1:17	3:17	5:19	7:19	8:35	9:17	11:17
46.9		Ar San Jose	9:28	11:25	1:25	3:25	5:28	7:28	8:43	9:25	11:25
	🚌	Ar Santa Cruz	10:30	12:30	2:30	4:30	6:40	8:30		10:30	

🚌 Indicates bus connection to Santa Cruz.

* New Year's Day, Memorial Day, Independence Day, Labor Day, Thanksgiving Day and Christmas Day. (CalTrain may operate reduced service on holiday eves and day after Thanksgiving). Call the CalTrain Hotline for details.

● Special train service during racing, football, Giants baseball seasons only.

Technology

Researching an Oil Spill:
A Library Computer Search
BOOK SEARCH

1

What would you like to find in the catalog?

EXXON VALDEZ

EXXON occurs 38 times in the catalog.

VALDEZ occurs 60 times in the catalog.

Searching Catalog!

2

Occurrences of: EXXON VALDEZ

Exxon Valdez (Ship)	Subject	
In the wake of the **Exxon Valdez:** the devastating impact of the Alaska oil spill/Art Davidson.	Title	1
Out of the channel: the **Exxon Valdez** oil spill in Prince William Sound/ John Keeble.	Title	1
Spill!: the story of the **Exxon Valdez**/ Terry Carr.	Title	1

END OF OCCURRENCES

Press ▲ or ▼ to view the occurrences then press **ENTER** to select.

Press **SAVE ITEM** to save a record.

3

Title selected: Spill!: the story of the Exxon Valdez/Terry Carr.

Title: Spill!: the story of the Exxon Valdez.
Author: Carr, Terry.
Publisher: New York: F. Watts, c1991.
Collation: 64 p.:ill.; 27 cm.
Subject: Exxon Valdez (Ship).
Subject: Oil spills--Environmental aspects-- Alaska--Prince William Sound Region.
Locations: Central Library: Children's Room. J 363.73C

Press ► or ◄ to browse other books.

To save or print this item, press one of the green keys at top of keyboard.

MAGAZINE SEARCH

=== **Search Screen** ===

Type the words to look for in the line below

Word(s) to look for: Exxon Valdez

Limit the search using the following fields

Magazine name:
Number of pages:
Date range:

Search for articles with illustrations (Y): Y
Search cover stories only (Y):

F1: help   **F2:** search   **F9:** clear all fields

①

=== **Result List in Date Order** ===

JAN 94-MAR 95

7. **Subject:** Oil spills--Alaska--Prince William Sound--Cleaning
    Title: New chemical digs deep into Exxon Valdez oil.
    Source: (National Geographic, Aug 94, Vol 186, Issue 2)

8. **Subject:** Oil spills--Prevention
    Title: Dress rehearsal for disaster. By Slater, Dashka
    Source: (Sierra, May/Jun 94, Vol 79, Issue 3)

JUL 92-DEC 93

9. Subject: Oil spills--Alaska
    Title: Frustrated fishermen block oil tankers.
    Source: (Alaska, Dec 93/Jan 94, Vol 59, Issue 11)

                                   Found: 156 items

Enter: display summary **F2:** select **F3:** modify search
F5: menu

②

GLOS

This glossary can help you to pronounce and find out the meanings of words in this book that you may not know.

The words are listed in alphabetical order. Guide words at the top of each page tell you the first and last words on the page.

Each word is divided into syllables. The way to pronounce each word is given next. You can understand the pronunciation respelling by using the key at right. A shorter key appears at the bottom of every other page.

When a word has more than one syllable, a dark accent mark (') shows which syllable is stressed. In some words, a light accent mark (') shows which syllable has a less heavy stress.

Glossary entries are based on entries in *The Macmillan/McGraw-Hill School Dictionary 1.*

a at, bad	**d** dear, soda, bad
ā ape, pain, day, break	**f** five, defend, leaf, off, cough, elephant
ä father, car, heart	
âr care, pair, bear, their, where	**g** game, ago, fog, egg
e end, pet, said, heaven, friend	**h** hat, ahead
ē equal, me, feet, team, piece, key	**hw** white, whether, which
i it, big, English, hymn	**j** joke, enjoy, gem, page, edge
ī ice, fine, lie, my	**k** kite, bakery, seek, tack, cat
îr ear, deer, here, pierce	**l** lid, sailor, feel, ball, allow
o odd, hot, watch	**m** man, family, dream
ō old, oat, toe, low	**n** not, final, pan, knife
ô coffee, all, taught, law, fought	**ng** long, singer, pink
ôr order, fork, horse, story, pour	**p** pail, repair, soap, happy
oi oil, toy	**r** ride, parent, wear, more, marry
ou out, now	**s** sit, aside, pets, cent, pass
u up, mud, love, double	**sh** shoe, washer, fish, mission, nation
ū use, mule, cue, feud, few	**t** tag, pretend, fat, button, dressed
ü rule, true, food	**th** thin, panther, both
u̇ put, wood, should	**th** this, mother, smooth
ûr burn, hurry, term, bird, word, courage	**v** very, favor, wave
	w wet, weather, reward
ə about, taken, pencil, lemon, circus	**y** yes, onion
b bat, above, job	**z** zoo, lazy, jazz, rose, dogs, houses
ch chin, such, match	**zh** vision, treasure, seizure

A

absorb To soak up or take in. A towel *absorbed* the spilled water.
ab•sorb (ab sôrb′ *or* ab zôrb′) *verb,* **absorbed, absorbing.**

Amazon The longest river in South America and, by volume, the largest in the world, flowing from the Andes across Brazil into the Atlantic. Its length is about 4,000 mi. (6,436 km).
Am•a•zon (am′ə zon′) *noun.*

ancestor A person from whom one is descended. Your grandparents and great-grandparents are among your *ancestors.*
an•ces•tor (an′ses tər) *noun,* *plural* **ancestors.**

Word History

The word **ancestor** comes from the French word *ancêtre* with the same meaning. This French word comes from the Latin words *ante-*, meaning "before" and *cēdere*, meaning "to go."

---

appear 1. To come into sight; be seen. The snowy mountain peaks *appeared* in the distance. **2.** To give the impression of being; look. They *appeared* interested in the game, but they were really bored.
ap•pear (ə pîr′) *verb,* **appeared, appearing.**

appreciate 1. To understand the value of. Everyone *appreciates* loyal friends. **2.** To be grateful for something. I *appreciate* your running these errands for me.
ap•pre•ci•ate (ə prē′shē āt′) *verb,* **appreciated, appreciating.**

aquarium 1. A tank, bowl, or similar container in which fish, other water animals, and water plants are kept. An aquarium is usually made of glass or some other material that one can see through. **2.** A building used to display collections of fish, other water animals, and water plants.
a•quar•i•um (ə kwar′ē əm) *noun,* *plural* **aquariums.**

aquarium

argue 1. To have a difference of opinion; disagree. My parents always *argue* about politics. **2.** To give reasons for or against something. I *argued* against going to the beach because it looked like it might rain.
ar•gue (är′gū) *verb,* **argued, arguing.**

arrangements Plans or preparations. Our class made *arrangements* to visit the zoo.
ar•range•ments (ə rānj′mənts) *plural noun.*

assorted Of many kinds. The bakery has a display of *assorted* cookies.
as•sort•ed (ə sôr′tid) *adjective.*

B

bamboo A tall plant that is related to grass. The bamboo has woody stems that are often hollow and are used to make fishing poles, canes, and furniture. *Noun.*
—Made of *bamboo. Adjective.*
   bam•boo (bam bü′) *noun, plural* **bamboos;** *adjective.*

Word History

The word **bamboo** comes from the Malay word *bambu* for the same plant.

bamboo

Bapa Raja (bä′pə rä′jə).

beneath 1. Lower than; below; under. We stood *beneath* the stars. 2. Unworthy of. Telling a lie is *beneath* you.
   be•neath (bi nēth′) *preposition.*

bore To make a hole in. The carpenter *bored* the wood with a drill. ▲ Another word that sounds like this is **boar.**
   bore (bôr) *verb,* **bored, boring.**

bough A large branch of a tree. We fastened the swing to a *bough* of the tree. ▲ Two other words that sound like this are **bow** (verb) and **bow** (noun).
   bough (bou) *noun, plural* **boughs.**

bound¹ 1. To leap; spring; jump. The rabbit *bounded* away into the woods. 2. To spring back after hitting something. The ball *bounded* off the wall and hit my bicycle.
   bound (bound) *verb,* **bounded, bounding.**

bound² 1. Fastened; tied. The bank robbers left the guard *bound* and gagged. 2. Have a duty or responsibility. I am *bound* by my promise to keep the secret.
   bound (bound) *adjective.*

Buddhist Relating to Buddhism, a religion that is based on the teachings of Buddha, an Indian religious leader who lived from about 563 B.C. to about 483 B.C.
   Bud•dhist (bùd′ist *or* bü′dist) *adjective.*

buffalo A large North American animal that has a big hump on its back; bison. Many years ago *buffalo* roamed free on the plains.
   buf•fa•lo (buf′ə lō) *noun, plural* **buffaloes** or **buffalos** or **buffalo.**

---

at; āpe; fär; câre; end; mē; it; īce; pîerce; hot; ōld; sông; fôrk; oil; out; up; ūse; rüle; pùll; tûrn; chin; sing; shop; thin; **th**is; hw in white; zh in treasure. The symbol ə stands for the unstressed vowel sound in about, taken, pencil, lemon, and circus.

C

cactus A plant that has a thick stem covered with spines instead of leaves. Cacti are found in desert areas of North and South America. Most cacti produce bright flowers and edible fruit.
    cac•tus (kak′təs) *noun, plural* **cacti** (kak′tī), **cactuses,** or **cactus.**

cactus

Camila (kä mē′lä).

Caracas The capital and largest city of Venezuela, in the northern part of the country.
    Ca•rac•as (kə rä′kəs).

Carlitos (kär lē′tōs).

catalogue A list. Stores publish catalogues with pictures and prices of the things they have for sale.
    cat•a•logue (kat′ə lôg′) *noun, plural* **catalogues.**

cellar A room or group of rooms built underground. Most *cellars* are under buildings and are used for storage.
    cel•lar (sel′ər) *noun, plural* **cellars.**

Cheo (chā′ō).

Chew and swallow (chü′ ənd swol′ō).

command 1. To give an order to; direct. The trainer commanded the dog to sit still. **2.** To have power over; rule. The general *commands* the army.
    com•mand (kə mand′) *verb,* **commanded, commanding.**

committee A group of persons who are chosen to do certain work. The decorations committee decorated the gym for the school dance.
    com•mit•tee (kə mit′ē) *noun, plural* **committees.**

community 1. A group of different plants and animals that live together in the same area and depend on one another for their survival. **2.** A group of people who live together in the same place. Our *community* voted to build a new library.
    com•mu•ni•ty (kə mū′ni tē) *noun, plural* **communities.**

company 1. Companionship. When the rest of the family is away, I am grateful for my dog′s *company.* **2.** A guest or guests. **3.** A business firm or organization. My father′s *company* is located in New York.
    com•pa•ny (kum′pə nē) *noun, plural* **companies.**

complicated Hard to understand or do. The directions for putting together the bicycle were too *complicated* for me to follow.
    com•pli•cat•ed (kom′pli kā′tid) *adjective.*

cooperate To work together. The three classes *cooperated* in planning a picnic at the end of the school year.
 co•op•er•ate (kō op′ə rāt′) *verb*, **cooperated, cooperating.**

Word History

The word **cooperate** comes from *co-*, a Latin word beginning that means "together," and the Latin word *operari*, meaning "to work."

---

coral A hard substance that is like stone and is found in tropical seas. Coral is made up of the skeletons of tiny sea animals. *Noun.*
—Made of *coral*. A *coral* reef surrounds the island. *Adjective.*
 cor•al (kôr′əl) *noun; adjective.*

coral

creature A living person or animal. Deer, bears, and wolves are *creatures* of the forest.
 crea•ture (krē′chər) *noun, plural* **creatures.**

crouch To stoop or bend low with the knees bent. The cat *crouched* in the bushes.
 crouch (krouch) *verb,* **crouched, crouching.**

curious Eager to learn about things that are new, strange, or interesting. I was really *curious* about those dinosaur bones.
 cu•ri•ous (kyur′ē əs) *adjective.*

customer A person who buys something at a store or uses the services of a business. Most of the bakery's regular *customers* shop there at least once a week.
 cus•tom•er (kus′tə mər) *noun, plural* **customers.**

D

damage Harm or injury that makes something less valuable or useful. The flood caused great *damage* to the farms in the area.
 dam•age (dam′ij) *noun, plural* **damages.**

dare **1.** To be bold enough to try; have the courage for. No one *dared* to go into the dark cave. **2.** To ask someone to do something as a test of courage or ability; challenge.
 dare (dâr) *verb,* **dared, daring.**

dedicate To set apart or devote to a special purpose or use. Many scientists have *dedicated* themselves to finding a cure for cancer.
 ded•i•cate (ded′i kāt′) *verb,* **dedicated, dedicating.**

---

at; āpe; fär; câre; end; mē; it; īce; pîerce; hot; ōld; sông; fôrk; oil; out; up; ūse; rüle; pùll; tûrn; chin; sing; shop; thin; this; hw in white; zh in treasure. The symbol ə stands for the unstressed vowel sound in about, taken, pencil, lemon, and circus.

---

demand To ask for urgently or forcefully. The customers *demanded* their money back for the broken radio.
> **de•mand** (di mand') *verb,* **demanded, demanding.**

depend **1.** To rely or trust. You can always *depend* on my friend to be on time. **2.** To get help or support. Children *depend* on their parents. **3.** To be determined by how something else turns out. Whether we go on the hike *depends* on the weather.
> **de•pend** (di pend') *verb,* **depended, depending.**

desert[1] A hot, dry, sandy area of land with few or no plants growing on it.
> **des•ert** (dez'ərt) *noun, plural* **deserts.**

desert

desert[2] To go away and leave a person or thing that should not be left; abandon. The soldiers *deserted* their company.
> **de•sert** (di zûrt') *verb,* **deserted, deserting.**

destroy To ruin completely; wreck. The earthquake *destroyed* the city.
> **de•stroy** (di stroi') *verb,* **destroyed, destroying.**

determined Firm in sticking to a purpose. The *determined* students kept phoning the senator's office until somebody answered.
> **de•ter•mined** (di tûr'mind) *adjective.*

develop **1.** To come gradually into being. A rash *developed* on the baby's skin. **2.** To grow or cause to grow; expand. You can *develop* your muscles by exercising.
> **de•vel•op** (di vel'əp) *verb,* **developed, developing.**

discuss To talk over; speak about. We *discussed* our favorite book.
> **dis•cuss** (di skus') *verb,* **discussed, discussing.**

drench To make something completely wet; soaked. The big wave *drenched* the children on the raft.
> **drench** (drench) *verb,* **drenched, drenching.**

echo The repeating of a sound. Echoes are caused when sound waves bounce off a surface. We shouted "hello" toward the hill and soon heard the *echo* of our voices.
> **ech•o** (ek'ō) *noun, plural* **echoes.**

election The act of choosing by voting. There is an *election* for the president every four years in the United States.
> **e•lec•tion** (i lek'shən) *noun, plural* **elections.**

environment 1. The air, the water, the soil, and all the other things that surround a person, animal, or plant. The *environment* can affect the growth and health of living things. **2.** Surroundings; atmosphere. The library provided a quiet *environment* for me to work.
　　en•vi•ron•ment (en vī′ rən mənt *or* en vī′ərn mənt) *noun, plural* **environments.**

especially More than usual. Be *especially* careful to not slip on the icy sidewalk.
　　es•pe•cial•ly (e spesh′ə lē) *adverb.*

exclaim To speak or shout suddenly, or with force; to express surprise or other strong feeling. "My bicycle's missing!" I *exclaimed.*
　　ex•claim (ek sklām′) *verb,* **exclaimed, exclaiming.**

Exxon Valdez (ek′son val dēz′ *or* väl dez′).

flutter To move or fly with quick, light, flapping movements. Butterflies *fluttered* among the flowers.
　　flut•ter (flut′ər) *verb,* **fluttered, fluttering.**

flutter

frequent Happening often; taking place again and again. There are *frequent* thunderstorms in this area.
　　fre•quent (frē′kwənt) *adjective.*

gaze To look at something a long time. We *gazed* at the sunset.
　　gaze (gāz) *verb,* **gazed, gazing.**

generation One step in the line of descent from a common relative. A grandparent, parent, and child make up three *generations.*
　　gen•er•a•tion (jen′ə rā′shən) *noun, plural* **generations.**

gradual Happening little by little; moving or changing slowly. We watched the *gradual* growth of the plants in our vegetable garden.
　　grad•u•al (graj′ü əl) *adjective.*

hesitate To wait or stop a moment, especially because of feeling unsure. The speaker *hesitated* and looked down at his notes.
　　hes•i•tate (hez′i tāt′) *verb,* **hesitated, hesitating.**

at; **ā**pe; f**ä**r; c**â**re; **e**nd; m**ē**; **i**t; **ī**ce; p**î**erce; h**o**t; **ō**ld; s**ô**ng; f**ô**rk; **oi**l; **ou**t; **u**p; **ū**se; r**ü**le; p**ů**ll; t**û**rn; **ch**in; si**ng**; **sh**op; **th**in; **th**is; **hw** in **wh**ite; **zh** in trea**s**ure. The symbol **ə** stands for the unstressed vowel sound in **a**bout, tak**e**n, penc**i**l, lem**o**n, and circ**u**s.

hoarse Having a deep, rough, or harsh sound. The teacher's voice was *hoarse* from a bad cold. ▲ Another word that sounds like this is **horse**.
> **hoarse** (hôrs) *adjective,* **hoarser, hoarsest.**

hollow **1.** Having a hole or an empty space inside; not solid. A water pipe is *hollow.* **2.** Curved in like a cup or bowl; sunken.
> **hol•low** (hol′ō) *adjective,* **hollower, hollowest.**

honor To show or feel great respect for a person or thing. The city *honored* the president with a parade.
> **hon•or** (on′ər) *verb,* **honored, honoring.**

imagine **1.** To picture a person or thing in the mind. Try to *imagine* a dragon breathing fire. **2.** To suppose; guess. I don't *imagine* we will go on a picnic if it rains.
> **i•mag•ine** (i maj′in) *verb,* **imagined, imagining.**

immediately Right away; now. If we leave *immediately,* we can get to the movie in time.
> **im•me•di•ate•ly** (i mē′dē it lē) *adverb.*

innocent **1.** Not doing harm; harmless. The children hid from their parents as an *innocent* joke. **2.** Free from guilt or wrong. An *innocent* person was accused of the crime, but a jury found the person not guilty.
> **in•no•cent** (in′ə sənt) *adjective.*

insect Any of a large group of small animals without a backbone. The body of an insect is divided into three parts. Insects have three pairs of legs and usually two pairs of wings. Flies, ants, grasshoppers, and beetles are *insects.*
> **in•sect** (in′sekt) *noun, plural* **insects.**

insect

insert To put or place in. I *inserted* a coin in the vending machine. *Verb.* —Something put or placed in. The Sunday edition of the newspaper has an eight-page color *insert* on vacations. *Noun.*
> **in•sert** (in sûrt′) *verb,* **inserted, inserting;** *noun, plural* **inserts.**

insist To demand or say in a strong, firm manner. The doctor *insisted* that the sick patient stayed in bed.
> **in•sist** (in sist′) *verb,* **insisted, insisting.**

intelligent Having or showing the ability to think, learn, and understand. *Intelligent* people often learn from their mistakes and do not repeat them.
    in•tel•li•gent (in tel′i jənt) *adjective.*

kapok A tropical tree that produces a light, fluffy fiber used as a stuffing for life preservers, pillows, and mattresses.
    ka•pok (kā′pok) *noun.*

kapok

Kitamura (ke tä mü′ rä).

jaguar A large animal that belongs to the cat family. The short fur of the jaguar is golden and is marked with black rings with spots in their centers. Jaguars are found in Mexico, Central America, and South America. The *jaguar* ran across the grassy plain.
    jag•uar (jag′wär) *noun, plural* **jaguars.**

Word History

The word **jaguar** comes from the Spanish word *yaguar* and the Portuguese word *jaguar,* which in turn came from the languages of the Guarani and Tupi Native Americans of the Amazon region.

---

jungle 1. Land in tropical areas that is covered with a thick mass of trees, vines, and bushes. Much of the Amazon River in Brazil runs through the dense *jungle.* **2.** Any wild, confused, or tangled growth or area. The city was a *jungle* of streets and skyscrapers.
    jun•gle (jung′gəl) *noun, plural* **jungles.**

Leonardo da Vinci 1452-1519, Italian artist and scientist. One of his most famous paintings is the *Mona Lisa.*
    Le•o•nar•do da Vin•ci (lē′ə när′dō də vin′chē) *noun.*

---

at; āpe; fär; câre; end; mē; it; īce; pîerce; hot; ōld; sông; fôrk; oil; out; up; ūse; rüle; pull; tûrn; chin; sing; shop; thin; **th**is; hw in **wh**ite; **zh** in trea**s**ure. The symbol ə stands for the unstressed vowel sound in **a**bout, tak**e**n, penc**i**l, lem**o**n, and circ**u**s.

---

librarian A person who is in charge of or works in a library. The *librarian* helped me find books for my report.
    li•brar•i•an (lī brâr′ē ən) *noun*, *plural* **librarians.**

memory 1. All that a person can remember. The student flawlessly recited the poem from *memory.* **2.** The ability to remember things. Maria has a good *memory.* **3.** A person or thing that is remembered. I have some good *memories* of my great-grandmother.
    mem•o•ry (mem′ə rē) *noun*, *plural* **memories.**

miracle 1. An amazing or wonderful thing. It was a *miracle* that our team won the championship. **2.** Something amazing or wonderful that cannot be explained by the laws of nature. It was a *miracle* she survived the shipwreck, because she cannot swim.
    mir•a•cle (mir′ə kəl) *noun*, *plural* **miracles.**

Miyo (mē′yō).

moist Slightly wet; damp. I wiped the shelves with a *moist* cloth.
    moist (moist) *adjective*, **moister, moistest.**

molecule The smallest particle into which a substance can be divided without being changed chemically. For example, a *molecule* of water has two atoms of hydrogen and one atom of oxygen.
    mol•e•cule (mol′ə kūl′) *noun*, *plural* **molecules.**

natural 1. Not resulting from teaching or training. The new sergeant was a *natural* leader. **2.** Found in nature; not made by people; not artificial. *Natural* rock formations overlook the river.
    nat•u•ral (nach′ər əl) *adjective.*

necessity Something that cannot be done without; requirement. Food, clothing, and shelter are the *necessities* of life.
    ne•ces•si•ty (ni ses′i tē) *noun*, *plural* **necessities.**

necklace A string of beads or other jewelry that is worn around the neck for decoration.
    neck•lace (nek′lis) *noun*, *plural* **necklaces.**

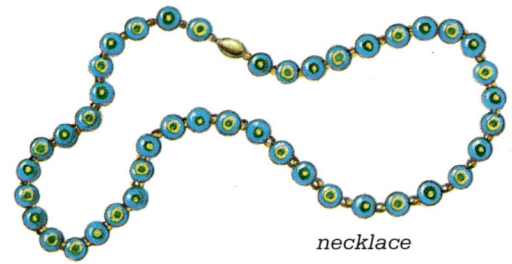

necklace

occasional Happening or appearing now and then; not frequent. The weather report said there will be *occasional* showers today.
    oc•ca•sion•al (ə kā′zhə nəl) *adjective.*

occur 1. To take place; happen. The fire *occurred* in the middle of the night. **2.** To come into one's thoughts. It did not *occur* to me to take my umbrella.
    oc•cur (ə kûr′) *verb,* **occurred, occurring.**

offer 1. The act of presenting something to be accepted or turned down. We accept your *offer* of help. **2.** Something presented to be accepted or turned down. The salesman turned down our *offer* of $500 for the old car.
    of•fer (ô′fər) *noun, plural* **offers.**

pardon 1. The act of refusing to blame or punish; forgiveness. I beg your *pardon* if I hurt you. **2.** A freeing from punishment. The prisoner received a *pardon* from the governor.
    par•don (pär′dən) *noun, plural* **pardons.**

particular 1. Taken by itself; apart from others. This *particular* suitcase is too small for me. **2.** Having to do with some one person or thing. This artist's *particular* talent is drawing plants. **3.** Unusual in some way; special. That book should be of *particular* interest to you.
    par•tic•u•lar (pər tik′yə lər) *adjective.*

perform 1. To carry out; do. The doctor *performed* the operation. **2.** To sing, act, or do something in public that requires skill. Our band *performed* at the game.
    per•form (pər fôrm′) *verb,* **performed, performing.**

permanent A wavy or curly hairdo that lasts several months, set in the hair with a chemical solution or with heat. *Noun.*
—Lasting or meant to last; enduring. After graduating from college, I started looking for a *permanent* job. *Adjective.*
    per•ma•nent (pûr′mə nənt) *noun; adjective.*

photograph A picture that is made by using a camera.
    pho•to•graph (fō′tə graf′) *noun, plural* **photographs.**

photograph

prediction The act of telling something before it happens. The weather *prediction* I heard on the radio said it would rain this weekend.
    pre•dic•tion (pri dik′shən) *noun, plural* **predictions.**

at; āpe; fär; câre; end; mē; it; īce; pîerce; hot; ōld; sông; fôrk; oil; out; up; ūse; rüle; pu̇ll; tûrn; chin; sing; shop; thin; this; hw in white; zh in treasure. The symbol ə stands for the unstressed vowel sound in about, taken, pencil, lemon, and circus.

prepare To make or get ready. We *prepared* for the race by doing some exercises.
pre•pare (pri pâr′) *verb*, **prepared, preparing.**

pretend 1. To give a false show. The children *pretended* to be asleep. **2.** To make believe. We *pretended* we were sailors on a large ship.
pre•tend (pri tend′) *verb*, **pretended, pretending.**

prevent 1. To keep something from happening. Putting out campfires helps *prevent* forest fires. **2.** To keep someone from doing something; hinder. The noise outside our window *prevented* us from sleeping.
pre•vent (pri vent′) *verb*, **prevented, preventing.**

prey 1. The habit of hunting animals for food. A tiger is a beast of *prey.* **2.** An animal that is hunted by another animal for food. Rabbits, birds, and snakes are the *prey* of foxes. ▲ Another word that sounds like this is **pray.**
prey (prā) *noun.*

prickly Having small, sharp thorns or points. We planted *prickly* rose bushes along the fence.
prick•ly (prik′lē) *adjective*, **pricklier, prickliest.**

produce 1. To make or create something. That factory *produces* automobiles. **2.** To bring forth; show. The lawyer *produced* new evidence at the trial.
pro•duce (prə düs′ *or* prə dūs′) *verb*, **produced, producing.**

pronounce 1. To make the sound of a letter or word. People from different parts of the country *pronounce* certain words differently. **2.** To say or declare. The judge *pronounced* the prisoner not guilty.
pro•nounce (prə nouns′) *verb*, **pronounced, pronouncing.**

quantity A number or amount. That restaurant buys large *quantities* of food.
quan•ti•ty (kwon′ti tē) *noun*, *plural* **quantities.**

Word History

The word **quantity** comes from the French word *quantité*, which in turn came from the Latin word *quantus*, meaning "how much" or "how large."

rescue To save or free. The lifeguard *rescued* the drowning child.
res•cue (res′kū) *verb*, **rescued, rescuing.**

ruins The remains of something destroyed or decayed. They found the *ruins* of an old stone wall.
ru•ins (rü′inz) *plural noun*

Chichén Itzá ruins

Rumphius (rum′fē əs).

S

San José (san hō zā′).

satisfaction The condition of being given, or the act of giving enough to meet one's needs or desires. Don't you get a lot of *satisfaction* from doing your homework well?
sat•is•fac•tion (sat′is fak′shən) *noun.*

scatter To spread or throw about in many different places. The wind *scattered* the leaves.
scat•ter (skat′ər) *verb,* **scattered, scattering.**

scowl To frown in an angry way. The father *scowled* at his child's rude behavior.
scowl (skoul) *verb,* **scowled, scowling.**

scrub To rub in order to wash or clean. You'll have to *scrub* your hands to get them clean.
scrub (skrub) *verb,* **scrubbed, scrubbing.**

scurry To go or move in a hurry. The children *scurried* after their parents.
scur•ry (skûr′ē) *verb,* **scurried, scurrying.**

seashore The land near or on the sea. We walked along the *seashore* and collected many beautiful shells.
sea•shore (sē′shôr′) *noun, plural* **seashores.**

Senhor Sir; mister. The Portuguese form of polite address for a man. The Portuguese language is spoken in Portugal, Brazil, and other countries.
se•nhor (si nyōr′ *or* si nyôr′) *noun.*

shaggy Long, bushy, and rough. That dog's hair is very *shaggy.*
shag•gy (shag′ē) *adjective,* **shaggier, shaggiest.**

shaggy

shelter To cover or protect. The tent *sheltered* us.
shel•ter (shel′tər) *verb,* **sheltered, sheltering.**

silent **1.** Completely quiet; still. She crept through the *silent* house. **2.** Not speaking, or saying little. The children remained *silent* during the play.
si•lent (sī′lənt) *adjective.*

species A group of animals or plants that have many characteristics in common. Poodles and beagles belong to the same *species.*
spe•cies (spē′shēz) *noun, plural* **species.**

at; āpe; fär; câre; end; mē; it; īce; pîerce; hot; ōld; sông; fôrk; oil; out; up; ūse; rüle; pu̇ll; tûrn; chin; sing; shop; thin; this; hw in white; zh in treasure. The symbol ə stands for the unstressed vowel sound in about, taken, pencil, lemon, and circus.

G13

squawk 1. To make a shrill, harsh cry like that of a frightened chicken. The parrot *squawked* when I waved a cracker in front of it. **2.** To complain loudly or harshly. Don't *squawk* about your chores.
> **squawk** (skwôk) *verb*, **squawked, squawking.**

startle To excite or cause to move suddenly, as with surprise or fright. A spider dropped from the ceiling and *startled* me.
> **star•tle** (stär′təl) *verb*, **startled, startling.**

suggest 1. To offer as something to think about. Who *suggested* that we play baseball? **2.** To come or bring into the mind. The color red *suggests* warmth. **3.** To hint. Your smile *suggests* that you are happy.
> **sug•gest** (səg jest′ *or* sə jest′) *verb*, **suggested, suggesting.**

Sun Ho (sun hō).

supply To provide with something needed or wanted. Rain *supplies* water. *Verb.*
—A quantity of something that is needed or ready for use. We have bought the *supplies* for our camping trip. *Noun.*
> **sup•ply** (sə plī′) *verb*, **supplied, supplying;** *noun, plural* **supplies.**

suspend 1. To attach so as to hang down. The swing was *suspended* from a branch. **2.** To support while allowing movement. Bits of lemon were *suspended* in the lemonade.
> **sus•pend** (sə spend′) *verb*, **suspended, suspending.**

Word History
The word **suspend** comes from the Latin word *suspendere*, which is made up of *sus-*, a Latin word beginning that means "up," and the Latin word *pendere*, meaning "to cause to hang."

Tami (tä′ mē).

temple[1] A building that is used for the worship of a god or gods. Long ago, the Romans built this *temple* as a place to pray to their gods.
> **tem•ple** (tem′pəl) *noun, plural* **temples.**

temple

temple[2] The flattened part on either side of the forehead. The *temple* is above the cheek and in front of the ear.
> **tem•ple** (tem′pəl) *noun, plural* **temples.**

twilight The time just after sunset or just before sunrise when there is a soft, hazy light.
> **twi•light** (twī′līt) *noun.*

twist 1. To wind or turn around something. The dog's chain was *twisted* around the tree. **2.** To change the meaning of; distort. He *twisted* our words.
　　twist (twist) *verb*, **twisted, twisting.**

valuable 1. Having great use or importance. My summer job was a *valuable* experience for me. **2.** Worth much money. The museum has a very *valuable* collection of paintings.
　　val•u•a•ble (val'ū ə bəl *or* val'yə bəl) *adjective*.

Venezuela A country in northern South America.
　　Ven•e•zue•la (ven'ə zwā'lə or ven'ə zwē'lə) *noun*.

Venezuela

vent A hole or other opening through which a gas or liquid passes in order to get out of somewhere. A *vent* above the stove lets air out of the kitchen.
　　vent (vent) *noun, plural* **vents.**

volunteer A person who offers to help, or does something by choice, and often without pay. The teacher asked for *volunteers* for the book fair committee. *Noun*
—**1.** To offer to help or do something of one's own free will. My friend *volunteered* to coach the baseball team. **2.** To give or offer readily. I *volunteered* an answer to the question. *Verb*.
　　vol•un•teer (vol'ən tîr') *noun, plural* **volunteers;** *verb* **volunteered, volunteering.**

warning Notice or advice given beforehand of a danger or possible bad result. The *warning* on the label said the bottle contained poison.
　　warn•ing (wôr'ning) *noun, plural* **warnings.**

whimper To cry with weak broken sounds. The puppy *whimpered* for it's mother
　　whim•per (hwim'pər *or* wim'pər) *verb*, **whimpered, whimpering.**

at; āpe; fär; câre; end; mē; it; īce; pîerce; hot; ōld; sông; fôrk; oil; out; up; ūse; rüle; pùll; tûrn; chin; sing; shop; thin; this; hw in white; zh in treasure. The symbol ə stands for the unstressed vowel sound in about, taken, pencil, lemon, and circus.

whirl To turn or cause to turn quickly in a circle. The blades of a fan *whirl* and create a cooling breeze.
> **whirl** (hwûrl *or* wûrl) *verb,* **whirled, whirling.**

wither To dry up and become wrinkled. Put the cut flowers in water before they *wither.*
> **with•er** (wi<u>th</u>′ər) *verb,* **withered, withering.**

Yanomamo A tribe of people who live in the rain forest of Brazil.
> **Ya•no•ma•mo** (yä′nō mä′mō) *noun.*

Young Mee (yung mē).

ACKNOWLEDGMENTS

The publisher gratefully acknowledges permission to reprint the following copyrighted material:

"All the Ones They Call Lowly" by David Campbell from A CARIBBEAN DOZEN. Edited by John Agard & Grace Nichols. Illustrations © 1994 Cathie Felstead. Permission granted by Walker Books Limited, London. Published in the U.S. by Candlewick Press, Cambridge, MA.

"And my heart soars" by Chief Dan George. Copyright © 1974 by Chief Dan George and Helmut Hirnschall. Reprinted by permission of Hancock House Publishing Ltd. 19313 Zeroz Ave., Surrey, BC V3S 5J9, Canada.

Illustration reprinted with permission of Atheneum Books for Young Readers, an imprint of Simon & Schuster from BEAT THE STORY-DRUM, PUM-PUM retold and illustrated by Ashley Bryan. Copyright (c) 1980 Ashley Bryan.

"Cactus Hotel" from CACTUS HOTEL text by Brenda Z. Guiberson, illustrated by Megan Lloyd. Text copyright © 1991 by Brenda Guiberson. Illustrations copyright © 1991 by Megan Lloyd. Reprinted by permission of Henry Holt and Co.

"Cloudy With a Chance of Meatballs" is from CLOUDY WITH A CHANCE OF MEATBALLS by Judi Barrett. Text copyright (c) 1978 by Judi Barrett. Illustrations copyright (c) 1978 by Ron Barrett. Reprinted with permission of Atheneum Books for Young Readers, Simon & Schuster Children's Publishing Division.

Illustration reprinted with permission of Atheneum Books for Young Readers, an imprint of Simon & Schuster from THE DANCING GRANNY retold and illustrated by Ashley Bryan. Copyright (c) 1977 by Ashley Bryan.

"Dream Wolf" is from DREAM WOLF by Paul Goble. Copyright © 1990 by Paul Goble. Reprinted with the permission of Simon & Schuster Books For Young Readers.

"A Fruit & Vegetable Man" from A FRUIT & VEGETABLE MAN by Roni Schotter. Text Copyright © 1993 by Roni Schotter; Illustrations copyright © 1993 by Jeanette Winter. By permission of Little, Brown and Company.

Cover reprinted with the permission of Simon & Schuster Books For Young Readers from THE GIRL WHO LOVED WILD HORSES by Paul Goble. Copyright 1978 by Paul Goble.

"Gone" from ONE AT A TIME by David McCord. Copyright © 1970 by David McCord. By permission of Little, Brown and Company.

"The Great Kapok Tree" from THE GREAT KAPOK TREE: A TALE OF THE AMAZON RAIN FOREST, copyright © 1990 by Lynne Cherry, reprinted by permission of Harcourt Brace & Company.

"An Incredible Journey" Water cycle board game adapted from "An Incredible Journey" in the Project Wet Curriculum and Activity Guide, a publication of Project WET. Illustration by Peter Grosshauer.

"In Memory" by Ericka Northrop from JACK AND JILL, copyright © 1989 by Children's Better Health Institute, Benjamin Franklin Literary & Medical Society, Inc., Indianapolis, Indiana. Used by permission.

"In Time of Silver Rain" from SELECTED POEMS by Langston Hughes. Copyright © 1938 and renewed 1966 by Langston Hughes. Reprinted by permission of Alfred A. Knopf Inc.

Cover permission for ISLAND BOY by Barbara Cooney. Copyright © 1988 by Barbara Cooney Porter. Used by permission by Viking Penguin, a division of Penguin Books, USA Inc.

Illustration from LION AND THE OSTRICH CHICKS retold and illustrated by Ashley Bryan. Copyright © 1986 Ashley Bryan. Reprinted with permission of Atheneum Books for Young Readers, an imprint of Simon & Schuster Children's Publishing Division.

"Miss Rumphius" from MISS RUMPHIUS by Barbara Cooney. Copyright © 1982 by Barbara Cooney Porter. Used by permission of Viking Penguin, a division of Penguin Books USA, Inc.

"Operation Rescue: Saving Sea Life from Oil Spills" by Christina Wilsdon. Copyright 1990 Children's Television Workshop (New York, New York). All rights reserved.

Cover permission for OX-CART MAN by Donald Hall, illustrated by Barbara Cooney. Copyright © 1979 by Barbara Cooney Porter for illustrations. Used by permission of Viking Penguin, a division of Penguin Books USA Inc.

"Preserven el Parque Elysian" by Mike Kellin. Copyright © 1965 (renewed) by APPLESEED MUSIC INC. All Rights Reserved. Used by Permission.

"Que llueva!"/"It's Raining" from ARROZ CON LECHE by Lulu Delacre. Copyright © 1989 by Lulu Delacre. English lyrics by Elena Paz. Reprinted by permission of Scholastic, Inc.

"Rain Forests Around the World" from WHY SAVE THE RAIN FOREST. Text © 1993 by Donald Silver. Illustrations © 1993 by Patricia Wynne. Silver Burdett Press, Simon & Schuster Elementary Group. Used by permission.

Text of "The Rains in Little Dribbles" from SOMETHING BIG HAS BEEN HERE by Jack Prelutsky. Copyright (c) 1990 by Jack Prelutsky. By permission of Greenwillow Books, a division of William Morrow and Company, Inc.

"The Rooster Who Understood Japanese" is from THE ROOSTER WHO UNDERSTOOD JAPANESE by Yoshiko Uchida. Text copyright © 1976 by Yoshiko Uchida. Reprinted courtesy of the Bancroft Library University of California, Berkeley.

"Spring Rain" is from RHYMES ABOUT US by Marchette Chute. Published 1974 by E.P. Dutton. Copyright © 1974 by Marchette Chute. Reprinted by permission of Elizabeth Roach.

"Storm in the Night" is from STORM IN THE NIGHT by Mary Stolz. Text copyright © 1988 by Mary Stolz. Illustrations copyright © 1988 by Pat Cummings. Reprinted by permission of HarperCollins Publishers.

"The Streets Are Free" is from THE STREETS ARE FREE/LA CALLE ES LIBRE by Kurusa, translation Karen Englander. Copyright © 1981 by Ediciones Ekare-Banco del Libro, Caracas, Venezuela. Used by permission of the publisher.

"The Toad" from SPEAKING OF COWS AND OTHER POEMS by Kaye Starbird. Copyright © 1960, © renewed 1988 by Kaye Starbird. Reprinted by permission of Marian Reiner for the author.

"Tornado Alert" from TORNADO ALERT by Franklyn M. Branley. Text copyright (c) 1988 by Franklyn M. Branley. Illustrations copyright (c) 1988 by Giulio Maestro. [Reprinted by permission of HarperCollins Publishers.

"Turtle Knows Your Name" is from TURTLE KNOWS YOUR NAME by Ashley Bryan. Copyright © 1989 by Ashley Bryan. Reprinted by permission of Atheneum Books for Young Readers, an imprint of Simon & Schuster Children's Publishing Division.

"Valentine for Earth" from THE LITTLE NATURALIST by Frances Frost. Copyright © 1959 by Frances Frost. Published by McGraw-Hill. Reprinted by permission.

"Volcanoes" by Judith E. Rand from NATIONAL GEOGRAPHIC WORLD, February 1995. Copyright © 1995 by National Geographic Society.

Illustration reprinted with the permission of Atheneum Books for Young Readers, an imprint of Simon & Schuster from WALK TOGETHER CHILDREN retold and illustrated by Ashley Bryan. Copyright (c) 1974 by Ashley Bryan.

"Weather Is Full of the Nicest Sounds" from I LIKE WEATHER by Aileen Fisher. Text copyright © 1963 by Aileen Fisher. By permission of the author, who controls rights..

"Weather Report" by Jane Yolen reprinted by permission of Curtis Brown Ltd. Copyright © 1992 by Jane Yolen. First appeared in WEATHER REPORT. Published by Boyds Mills Press.

"The Wolves of Winter" by Rachel Bucholz, photographs by Jim Brandenburg, from BOY'S LIFE, February 1995. Copyright © 1995 by Boy Scouts of America. Reprinted by permission.

READING RESOURCES

Diagrams: From WEATHER FORECASTING by Gail Gibbons, copyright © 1987 by Gail Gibbons. Reprinted by permission of Four Winds Press, an imprint of Simon & Schuster Books For Young Readers.

Maps: "Indian Groups of North America" from UNITED STATES AND ITS NEIGHBORS, copyright © 1991 by Macmillan/McGraw-Hill School Publishing Company. Reprinted by permission of Macmillan/McGraw-Hill School Publishing Company.

Schedules: Excerpt from CalTrain Peninsula Rail Service timetable. Reprinted by permission of the California Department of Transportation.

COVER DESIGN: Carbone Smolan Associates
COVER ILLUSTRATION: Daniel Adel (front - girl with umbrella), Timothy Raglin (front - mice), Marc Mongeau (back)

DESIGN CREDITS
Carbone Smolan Associates, front matter and unit openers
Bill Smith Studio, 72-73, 128-129,174-177, 222-225
Function Thru Form, Inc., 300-301, 306-311, 314, 316-317
Sheldon Cotler + Associates Editorial Group, 206-221, 226-267, 270-299
Notovitz Design Inc., 302-305, 312-313, 315

ILLUSTRATION CREDITS
Unit 1: Marc Mongeau, 10-11; Susan Huls, 12-13, 29 (borders); Claudia Karabaic Sargent, 32, 34-38, 40-46 (borders); Kathy Jeffers, 48-49 (valentine globe); Grace De Vito, 72-73 (title panel); Leo Kubinyi, 72-73 (map); Steven Bennett, 74 (calligraphy); Jose Ortega, 102-103.
Unit 2: Daniel Adel, 104-105; Douglas Scheider, 106; Andrea Eberbach, 130-131; Steven Bennett, 130, 180, 201 (calligraphy); Olivia, 158-159; Yemi, 160-161. **Unit 3:** Timothy Raglin, 204-205; Mary Collier, 221; SC & A, 226,229,231-232, 235 (logos); Steve Stankiewicz, 235; Greisbach & Martucci, 238-239; John Hamburger, 236-237; Gene Boyer, 270-271; David Goldin, 296-297 (border); Nicholas Fasciano, 296-297 (bkgd.).**Reading Resources:** Brad Hamann, 302, 312; Steve Stankiewicz, 305; Denny Bond, 306; Maria Lauricella, 308; Steve Sullivan, 309; Bob Mansfield, 310-311; Patrick Merrill, 313; Sean Daly,

316-317.**Glossary:** Lori Anzalone, G3, G4, G7, G8, G10, G13; Greg King, G15.

PHOTOGRAPHY CREDITS

The Test-Taker's
HANDBOOK

★ It's almost time to take a test.

★ Are you ready?

★ You can learn some strategies.

★ You can be a better test-taker.

How to Use This Handbook

Sometimes, taking a test can make you worried. These pages will help you feel better about taking tests.

On these pages, you will find information and hints to help with different kinds of questions. You will also learn how to use what you know to make taking tests a little easier. Sometimes jotting down a few words or making up rhymes or other games will help you remember the information.

This section will help with different kinds of tests. It will help with tests that your teacher gives you. It will also help you with special tests that you might have to take.

Before you take a test, look at this section again. Each time you read it, you will remember more about taking tests. That will help you become a better test-taker.

Hints for Taking Tests

Do you think that Mark McGwire practices before a big baseball game? Sure he does!

Before you take a test, you can practice, too.

Think about these hints and strategies. Practice as many of these as you can.

It Takes Practice

Practice to get in shape before a test.

FIND OUT

★ Ask your teacher what will be on the test.

★ Will it be a book test?

★ Will it be a special test, such as the SAT?

LOOK BACK

★ Check old tests. Look at old practice papers.

★ Review what you did right.

★ Make sure you understand what you did wrong.

The trains "sound like thunder" means that they

○ make a lot of noise.

○ cause rain.

○ make the stations clean.

○ flash with bright lights.

What came first in the passage?

○ The girl jumped into the water.

○ The boy swam across the lake.

○ The puppy jumped into the lake.

○ The puppy saved the girl.

What is the main idea of the first paragraph?

○ Animals are different from people.

○ Animals can't talk.

○ Scientists know how animals act.

○ Animals work together.

Show What You Know

Do you get a little nervous when you have to take a test? That's OK — it happens to many of us.

Take a deep breath and say, "I am ready. I can do this."

Sometimes it helps to think about work you have done before.

Review reading strategies that you already know.

Tick, Tick, Tick

Most tests are timed, but time can be on your side. Just play it smart.

- Take some time to study before the test.

- Skip items that you are not sure of. Come back to them later.

- Try to sum up the information. This will give you the main ideas.

Oh, I remember doing one like this for homework.

TRY:

★ rereading

★ looking for clue words

★ using other words in the sentence

★ thinking about synonyms

Hmm, I better check this answer again.

Double Check

- When you finish an item, ask yourself these questions:

  ☐ Is my answer reasonable?

  ☐ Did I answer the question?

- Try to find the answer in the passage.

Be Careful

I can't answer this. I don't have enough information.

You know better!

Use these hints to help you avoid common errors:

- Look for clue words in the question.

- Look for clue words in the answer choices.

- Use time-order words in the passage to help you.

- Watch for words that have more than one meaning. Use the other words in the sentence to help you.

My answer is not one of the choices.

This answer doesn't make sense, but it is one of the choices so it must be right.

The right answers have been first and third, so all the right answers must be first and third.

Preparing for Tests

A multiple-choice test can be the easiest kind of a test. Why? Because you know that one of the choices is the right answer. All you have to do is figure out which one it is.

- O three birds
- O two cats
- O one dog
- ● four ferrets

Remember to fill in only one circle for each question.

Completely fill in the correct circle for each item.

Damon and Leo stood by the lake.

"Dad, can we go swimming?" Damon asked. "The soccer game has made us really hot."

"It looks like rain," Dad answered. "Let's wait and see."

"Look," cried Theo, "the sun has come out!"

Reread the story.

1 Who wants to go swimming?
- O Mom
- O Dad
- O Damon and Leo
- O Dad and Damon

Sometimes answers don't make sense. Ignore those choices right away.

2 What have Damon and Leo just finished doing?
- O swimming
- O playing baseball
- O playing soccer
- O running around the lake

Practicing Reading Tests

Directions

Read the passage. Then read each question about the story. Choose the best answer to each question. Mark the space for the answer you have chosen.

Look for key words to help you find the answer.

Registration for Pine Valley Day Camp will be held on Saturday, May 3. The program includes daily swimming in the pond and the pool. There are nature hikes, arts and crafts, music, sports, and campfires. The camp accepts all children ages 4–12 who live in the town of Pine Valley.

Registration will be from 9:00 A.M. to 11:00 A.M. at the Pine Valley Town Hall. The sign-up fee is $10.

Use other words in the sentence to help you learn the meaning of a new word.

1 What is the meaning of registration?
- ○ Learning to swim
- ○ Singing songs
- ○ Signing up
- ○ Drawing pictures

2 Where can you register?
- ○ At the swimming pool
- ○ At the pond
- ○ At a campfire
- ○ At the town hall

Practicing Reading Tests

Directions

Read the letter. Then read each question about the letter. Choose the best answer to each question. Mark the space for the answer you have chosen.

Try to match words in the passage with words in the question.

Dear Sandy,

I'm taking Alice to the dentist. We should be home around 5:00. After you have done your homework, would you please start dinner? Spread the pizza dough onto a cookie sheet. Then pour the jar of sauce onto the dough. Sprinkle the cheese on top. I will turn on the oven when I get home.

Thanks,

Mom

3 What does spread mean in this passage?
- ○ A cover for a bed
- ○ What you put on bread
- ○ Cover the top of something
- ○ Move something apart

4 Which job will Mom do?
- ○ Pour the sauce
- ○ Turn on the oven
- ○ Spread the dough
- ○ Sprinkle the cheese

Skim the passage to help you find the answer.